Dead Kennedys

Fresh Fruit for Rotting Vegetables,
The Early Years

Dead Kennedys

Fresh Fruit for Rotting Vegetables,
The Early Years

Alex Ogg

Dead Kennedys: Fresh Fruit for Rotting Vegetables, The Early Years
Alex Ogg © 2014

This edition © 2014 PM Press

ISBN: 978-1-60486-489-2
LCCN: 2013956920

10 9 8 7 6 5 4 3

PM Press
P.O. Box 23912
Oakland, CA 94623

Book design by Russ Bestley • www.hitsvilleuk.com
Front cover design by John Yates • www.stealworks.com

DK Photographs (where specified) © Ruby Ray, Mick McGee
Fallout magazine © Winston Smith • www.winstonsmith.com

Printed in the USA

Acknowledgements

The author would like to dedicate this book to Dawn Nichola Wrench – 'Never TDTF'

He also thanks the staff and students at Brittons and in particular 10ad/en1 for contract-checking and 8OGG, his day job treasures.

Jello's support for this project was crucial in seeing it finally reach print, but the author also acknowledges the contributions made by his fellow band members when the project existed in a different guise. The author would also like to thank his favourite collage artist, Winston Smith, for his support and involvement in this project. Others who were vital to the development of the book included all those interviewed, and special thanks to Russ Bestley (design), Roger Sabin, Vanessa Demaude and Josef Loderer (for advice and encouragement), Helen Donlon (his fab literary agent), Mick McGee and Ruby Ray (for photos). Thanks also to DK record and memorabilia specialists Tony Raven, Mason Bermingham, Andrew Kenrick, Iain Scatterty, Vaughan Wyn Roberts, Darren Hardcastle, Kevin Shepherd and Rich Hassall for rare record cover details and images, and to Jay Allen Sanford of Rock 'n' Roll Comics. Vasilia Dimitrova brought her illustration skills to bear to highlight an essential part of the story, and thanks to Allan Kausch for initial editing and feedback, together with early gig flyers and information, and Gregory Nipper for an extremely detailed final edit. Thanks too to co-publishers Kristiina in Finland, Craig and Ramsey in America, Joachim in Germany, Maria in Brazil, David in the dear old UK and anyone who's been forgotten!

Contents

WINSTON SMITH 2013

FRESH FRUIT BOOK COVER
ALEX OGG

FRESH FRUIT BOOK COVER

Previous pages: Book jacket collages by Winston Smith, 2013.

𝔓𝔯𝔢𝔮𝔲𝔢𝔩
When Ya Get Drafted

ome of the interview material collated herein was originally commissioned as the basis for the projected sleeve notes to the twenty-fifth anniversary reissue of *Fresh Fruit For Rotting Vegetables*. The fact that said endeavour was derailed by wrangling among former members will come as no great surprise to longstanding observers of Dead Kennedys. The maxim is that history is dictated by the winners, whether said victory be defined by court case, fiscal arm-twisting, media access or variations on those themes. Efforts to maintain authorial independence on the project were undermined by warring factions competing over the narrative and in the end the sleeve notes were withdrawn. Or rather just tossed aside. The final stumbling block was *a single sentence*, which is retained in this book (you'll struggle to spot it though, it's astonishingly innocuous). It got very messy and at times deeply unpleasant. But it represents subject matter I was always committed to returning to. And it's taken to the *thirtieth* anniversary, and beyond, to sort it all out.

It was a salutary lesson in how deep some feuds run, and yet I maintain that it was a tragic denouement to a job well worth undertaking. Informed readers will doubtless be aware how much the reputation of the band has been tarnished over recent years. To borrow *San Francisco Chronicle* writer James Sullivan's analogy, any metaphysical statue the city might have erected in the band's honour just got covered in seagull poop. Yet a great band they truly were. I am not alone in ranking *Fresh Fruit* as one of the most important albums to emerge from punk, one of only a handful that genuinely transcended genre – stretching musical and lyrical conventions while making a point, or several dozen, and jabbing funny bones the world over. This is an effort to restore its standing. Or hose off some of the guano.

In fact, the history of this project extends even deeper than the sleeve-note debacle. In 1991 I was editing a British music magazine to which someone submitted an article on the band. I was very keen to publish, and sent it off to Dead Kennedys' singer Jello Biafra for evaluation and scrutiny. When he eventually replied there were over a hundred written amendments – he wasn't too taken by the writer. He wasn't all that impressed, either, when he discovered said magazine's publisher had bootlegged DKs records in the past – a fact I was blissfully unaware of at the time. In the event the magazine disappeared down the tubes. In effect, then, what you are reading has spent two decades in gestation. That sounds overly grand; I've applied myself to the odd job in between.

Our correspondence continued, albeit sporadically, over the course of two decades. Thereafter I was commissioned to submit an article on the band for another music magazine, and a similar process of writing and revision was embarked upon. Unfortunately, at that precise moment the legal shenanigans between the former band-mates erupted and the piece was lost in the shuffle. Another few years rolled by and in 2005 I was asked to write the aforementioned sleeve notes. I was thrilled, naively thinking I could get around entrenched positions by playing fair and being transparent to all parties. I spent about a month working with the former members on new interviews and got some great material. Then it got to the nitty gritty and pretty soon I was trying to mediate various issues, showing each party the other's replies and attempting to reconcile what could broadly, and generously, be described as competing takes on history.

The opposing parties by this point had diluted to Biafra versus guitarist East Bay Ray, which again will not be a surprising revelation to those who know something of the band's internal politics. Klaus Flouride (bass) very much follows Ray's lead in inter-band affairs and Ted, in charmingly typical drummer-like fashion, seemed completely bemused as to why anyone would wish to bother. I was pretty close to coming round to his way of thinking by the end.

Petty just doesn't cover it. The ten drafts wound up running to over sixty-four thousand words; we had space for five thousand. At one stage an employee at Alternative Tentacles (Dead Kennedys' record label subsequently administered by Biafra) complained that I'd single-handedly broken their printer. There was a lengthy telephone debate on whether to allow a band member the use of the personal rather than collective pronoun. As part of my increasingly desperate attempts at appeasement, I ended up totting up quote allocations to prove that everyone's thoughts were evenly accounted for.[1] If the men in white coats had knocked at my door at this stage, I would have gone quietly. The absolute nadir was when one band member – not Biafra – accused me of being the cause of his bad back. Over a transatlantic phone call. Repeatedly.

In the end it ran something like this. Biafra will chide and cajole and do his utmost to persuade you of the veracity of his interpretation of events. Then he will concede that you have the right to call it as you see it as a writer. Ray will chide and cajole and do his utmost to persuade you of the veracity of *his* interpretation of events. And then he will call his lawyer. The curse of the Kennedys? I must admit I am finalising the current manuscript with more than vague apprehension. What else could possibly go wrong?

For all that, I still adore the record. *Fresh Fruit For Rotting Vegetables* is not *London Calling*. It is not *Never Mind The Bollocks*, nor is it *The Ramones*. To me, it is superior to that lauded trio, mainly because of the lyrical and musical intelligence that underpins it, which utterly captivated and compelled back in 1980, scarily three decades ago. I could support this doubtless hysterical contention by pointing out that it regularly features in greatest punk album polls voted for by *the people* (though it should be noted that *the people* are a stupid bunch, by and large, as Sid Vicious once set out in rather more florid terms). The album's afterlife is such an extraordinary achievement for a band who had practically zero radio play and only released records on independent labels – no EMI, CBS or Warners for them. They not only existed outside of the mainstream but were, as V. Vale of *Search And Destroy* fanzine noted, the first band of their stature to turn on and *attack* the music industry itself. The DKs set so much in motion. They were integral to the formulation of an alternative American network that allowed bands on the first rung of the ladder to tour outside of their own backyard. They were instrumental in supporting the concept of all-ages shows and spurned the advances of corporate rock promoters and industry lapdogs. They legitimised the whole notion of an American punk band working successfully in the UK and Europe while disseminating the true horror of their native country's foreign policies; effectively serving as anti-ambassadors on their travels.

The record label they established, the still-thriving Alternative Tentacles, boasts as challenging a back-catalogue of musical extremity to service dysfunctional listening tastes as you could possibly desire. And the gallery of crooked politicians, charlatan preachers and corporate crocodiles they managed to provoke over the course of their career is unparalleled. How much are they part of the DNA of both punk and popular music? Although it's not scientific, Jack Black's *School of Rock* blackboard traces a straight line that runs Pistols-Ramones-Clash-Dead Kennedys. Biafra will have a right wobbly when I use *that* as justification. I'm a bit wobbly myself.

The aforementioned triumvirate – Pistols, Clash, Ramones – has collectively had more than a hundred books published in their name. The DKs have *never* been written about at length, or celebrated accordingly, despite *Fresh Fruit* selling over a quarter of a million records in Europe alone. Their own fault, really. They never *progressed* to make a *rock 'n' roll* record – conventional rock criticism continuing to hold that the punk genus is something intrinsically juvenile; at the very best a chrysalis stage. They also fell out spectacularly, meaning people tend to tread warily around demonstrably litigious elements in this story. And, in many ways, what they put on the record was more intractably *violent* towards public and critical perception. "Sure, I wanted the band to last," says Biafra. "But some of the best bands are the ones that go out of their way to shock and annoy people, and not just pander and please." Here's a story that gives credence to that statement.

Fresh Fruit arrived at a juncture when critics and opinion leaders had distanced themselves from punk, claiming primacy in its discovery but disdain of its subsequent trajectory – the school of thinking that suggests art is ruined at the moment it is consumed by more than a small cultural elite. The UK had three specialist music papers demanding a steady stream of flavours of the week. By the turn of the decade New Romanticism was the latest bag for the style-conscious, heavy metal was being readmitted to polite society for those bereft of such concerns, and punk was widely regarded as a victim of infant mortality. But an evolution was underway and a corrective overdue. For many who believed that the movement was more than a showy outcrop of the unhindered continuum of rock 'n' roll, *Fresh Fruit* confirmed punk's potential to stand for something beyond the trappings of fashion and faux rebellion.

The debate over punk etymology, whether it originated in CBGB's or St Martin's College of Art, is effectively asinine, but it's unarguable that by the late '70s the UK had shaped the discourse. By the turn of the '80s, however, Brit-punk was beginning to run on empty. Subject matter and stylistic form were contracting. Crass had politicised punk in a sharp rebuttal of The Clash, who had moved on to starry lights and stadiums, and the imploding Pistols. As Biafra himself notes, "Crass were trying to get punks to think and act beyond punk, that feeling good about buying an album called *Sandinista* did nothing to actually help anyone in Nicaragua." But for all their intelligence and sincerity, Crass were too abrasive, too austere to make a record of similar weight. Punk, at least in the UK, had become woefully po-faced and worthy; simply too obvious. As Al Spicer would write, when their debut record 'California Über Alles' was first spun by John Peel, "it sounded like nothing the British punk scene had heard before and was as refreshing and welcome as the bugle sound of the cavalry coming to the rescue."

Fresh Fruit offered a perfect hybrid of humour and polemic strapped to a musical chassis that was as tetchy and inventive as Biafra's withering broadsides. Those lyrics, cruel in their precision, were revelatory. But it wouldn't have worked if the underlying sonics were not such an uproarious rush, the paraffin to Biafra's naked flame. And if we can set aside the bickerfest for a fleeting moment, we can remember what a cool, funny, savage little record *Fresh Fruit For Rotting Vegetables* was.

I Left My Rights In San Francisco

Chapter 1

So You've Been to School for a Year or Two

It is an odd thing, but everyone who disappears is said
to be seen at San Francisco. It must be a delightful city,
and possess all the attractions of the next world.
(Oscar Wilde)

It's the Amerikan in me
that makes me watch the blood
Runnin' out of the bullet hole in his head
(The Avengers' 'The American In Me', referencing JFK's assassination)

San Francisco was a natural crucible for punk. For years it had been synonymous with liberal thought, with vocal gay rights, feminist and ecological lobbies, and in the '60s became a magnet to the Beats and base camp for the Summer of Love. It also had the working class districts one would associate with a port town. A haven, then, for weirdos, hippies and eccentrics, as well as more rational left-leaning thinkers, it was natural that, after New York, and alongside its Californian neighbour Los Angeles, it rejoiced in the punk ethos of difference. It was, after all, at the city's Winterland Ballroom that the Sex Pistols played their final show, not so much passing the baton as dropping it where they stood. Or, in Sid's case, fell over. "In San Francisco," notes singer Jello Biafra, "a lot of the prime movers of all the different things in the arts over the years came from people who came there from *somewhere else*. It's not like London or New York, where a lot of the people grew up there. It's a city where people are drawn from all over the country, and even the world, to chase their dream and find some freedom to try to see what they can become." A city that Paul Kantner of Jefferson Airplane once succinctly described as "Forty-nine square miles surrounded by reality". Any reference to the latter band in

Above left:...at the Mabuhay 1978. Audience after Crime's set – Biafra, Bruce Conner and Mindaugis Bagdon in the front row. (Photograph by Ruby Ray)
Below left: Avengers, live at the Mabuhay 1977. Penelope Houston, Greg Ingraham and Danny Furious. (Photograph by Ruby Ray)

a book about Dead Kennedys might provoke bewilderment, but the lineage back to the '60s was clear. The band itself was explicit. "We were trying to restore what the hippies believed in," guitarist East Bay Ray would state, "tolerance for experimentation, the do-it-yourself thing and the questioning of authority." "And," adds Biafra, "insurrection, direct action and good old-fashioned pranks."

If the city offered opportunity for innumerable square pegs, Frisco's traditional celebration of outsiders was also readily simpatico with punk values; the discarding of status built on appearance, wealth or career advancement. "Unlike London," Biafra points out, "San Francisco had no Carnaby Street or King's Road. Punk fashion throughout California was 98% DIY, straight out of charity shops. Look at old pictures of the Weirdos and The Dickies! Even the Hollywood punks got their gear from Salvation Army." Instead, San Franciscan punk made personal eccentricities a positive and baited the pomposity of those who would assume authority over others. Above all it fetishised individuality, personal creativity and self-expression. Mutual support and collaboration were key elements. One of punk's myths was that its year zero culture was effectively a big bang – an instant grow-bag with everyone at each other's throats – when in truth it scooped up those already disaffected and desperately waiting for something to happen, something the misfits and mis-shapes could belong to.

When Ray put up an advert ('guitarist wants to start punk or new wave band') in Aquarius Records, reprinted in San Francisco's *BAM* newspaper, he had a singular intention. He wanted to have the best such band in San Francisco. Which may not sound such a lofty ambition, but by the time the ad was placed in 1978, the city had already midwifed a hugely diverse punk generation.

Front-runners Crime and The Nuns delivered attitudinal, primal rock'n'roll and to this day dispute the honour of being the city's first punk band. Crime, who initially eschewed the punk tag, would take the stage dressed as cops, or in fedoras or tuxedos, play turbo-charged Stooges-like punk-blues at deafening volume with a sense of melodrama that recalled Kiss as much as MC5. They legendarily told Seymour Stein that he needed to get the Ramones a haircut. The Nuns, led by Jennifer Miro and featuring future alt-country star Alejandro Escovedo, were no less a force – the visual equivalent of Marlene Dietrich fronting the Dead Boys and for some time the movement's biggest live draw. They were the first San Francisco punk band to play an 'official' gig at the scene epicentre Mabuhay Gardens and the first to be courted by the majors, though in the end they elected to sign with Howie Klein's 415 when a deal with Columbia fell through. It was a harbinger of the fate that would befall all of the city's pioneering punk bands.

The Avengers, who alongside The Nuns supported the Pistols at Winterland, had a keen instinct for taut melody as well as aggression. With singer Penelope Houston as impossibly cool, photogenic lead, they led the second wave, but cruelly never got to release an album despite having material sufficient for three. Their peers included the highly theatrical, populous Mutants, who played alongside The Cramps at the State Mental Asylum in Napa, causing consternation among guards attempting to differentiate between performer and audience. The Dils, led by the Kinman brothers, had relocated from San Diego and established a class-themed political consciousness that would later be refined in the region's punk bible/ pre-internet punk networking compass *Maximum Rock 'n' Roll*. The swaggering Sleepers from Palo Alto, featuring Crime's original drummer Rickie Williams on vocals, a registered schizophrenic trailer-park live wire, referenced The Stooges but also mined SF's psychedelic (musical and pharmaceutical) hinterland, and were the Germs' Darby Crash's favourite band.

The insanely confrontational Negative Trend probably held the upper hand, however, in terms of envelope-pushing. In one of his last acts as manager of the 'real' Sex Pistols, Malcolm McLaren had asked them to headline above his charges at Winterland after enquiring as to the identity of the 'worst' band in the area. Original vocalist Rozz Rezabek left at the age of *seventeen*, the Bay Area's very own Iggy having burnt himself out physically. He had famously completed a show with a broken arm at the Iguana Studios before an indifferent Sandy Pearlman, renowned for producing Blue Öyster Cult but having just worked on The Clash's second album, *Give 'Em Enough Rope*. Indeed, he had not merely broken his arm, but actually gone to hospital then returned to the gig to break it again in a different place. Biafra unsuccessfully auditioned for the vacant spot. So too did Bruce Loose, who would eventually find a berth in fellow Negative Trend survivor Will Shatter's subsequent band, Flipper.

Dead Kennedys would arrive as part of a third wave spearheaded by The Offs, who blended buzz-saw guitar and Velvet Underground-styled drone-noise with dub bass. Incidentally this author does not claim to have been a witness to any of these bands. Fortuitously, Joe Rees at Target Video shot them all, providing the most comprehensive audio and visual catalogue of an emerging movement that any Johnny Latecomer could wish to access.

The shock of hearing Dead Kennedys therefore, at least outside San Francisco, has to be reconciled to this unique context. What made 'California Über Alles' and 'Holiday In Cambodia' sound more jarring, sarcastic and musically spiteful than the offspring of Lydon and Strummer was the result of a scene largely sealed from outside gaze in which the impetus to outdo, outperform and out-out was abroad. Not only had the city embraced punk, it had accelerated the process of personalising it.

All those storied groups, however, were forced to survive without any kind of infrastructure at a time when recording and independently releasing records remained a pipe dream. It was against this firmament of fast-evolving creative dissidence, and logistical obstacles, that any new San Franciscan punk band would have to measure itself.

Already a seasoned musician who had grown up on his dad's Duke Ellington collection, Ray, the band's sole Bay Area native, was inspired by Scotty Moore's guitar playing on Elvis's early records as well as Syd Barrett-era Pink Floyd. It was seeing the latter band play at Winterland in October 1970 as a twelve-year-old that convinced him to pick up a guitar. Later, he got into the Ohio Players when '70s rock started to chase its own tail. He was immediately excited by the arrival of the Ramones and the first English punk records he heard.[2] Ray had a caveat in reference to potential respondents to his advert. In defiance of prevailing notions, he wanted everyone to be not just proficient or capable, but individually excellent.

Raymond Pepperell, to use Ray's birth name, has a mathematics degree. "I graduated from University of California, Berkeley. So I have a right brain and a left brain. I forget which is which! I really respond to music, though, non-intellectually." His parents were both politically active. "They were involved in the civil rights movement, fighting block-busting in the '50s and '60s – people would put a black family in a block of white people, then buy up all the white houses cheap. And redlining insurance neighbourhoods [the practice of hiking insurance costs in predominantly black areas]. My parents were fighting that, too. My parents were definitely activists and liberals, particularly in civil rights. I know I got dragged to one or two protest meetings. My dad was even on the school board for a while. He worked at a corporation and wore a suit and tie, but was doing this stuff. Both mom and dad dressed strait-laced. But they weren't. My mom used to listen to Pete Seeger in The Weavers. And Frank Sinatra! Guilty pleasure!"

He was already an experienced if unfulfilled musician. "I only had six months of guitar lessons, and the teacher wasn't showing me what I wanted to know, so I mostly learned from records. In high school I played with friends and my brother played drums. That was in the suburbs of California [Castro Valley], still in the East Bay. I went to college and stopped playing. When I got out of college, I was playing in a bar band at the time, making $100 a week. I thought, I can live off this! So I was working three or four nights a week. It wasn't satisfying, but it was educational." The one document of this time is his contribution to the Bay Area showband Cruisin', who cut one single, 'Vicky's Hickey', which the band sold at shows through the mid-'70s. They even had alternate Beatles and Beach Boys sets, complete with swimming trunks.

By the time 1978 swung around, he had begun to notice punk stirring. "I'd heard of the Sex Pistols and Ramones, and I was listening to them. Then I went to see the Weirdos at the Mabuhay [Gardens]. One of the ways I like to test music is if the little hairs on the back of my neck stand on end. That happened when I saw the Weirdos live. 'Ah, this is what I want to do.' I was in the area having dinner and I wandered in and talked to them." Thereafter he put his plan in motion, but was determined that his new band's musicianship should be spurred rather than tethered by the punk breakout. Instinctively he rejected the 'two chords and the truth' mantra of UK punk. "Originally, when I put up the advertisements for the band, one of the images of punk was that you shouldn't be able to play your instrument, which is a bit of a myth. When I put the ad in, I said I wanted to start a punk band, but people *had to be able to play*."

The first respondent to the Aquarius advert was Eric Boucher, soon to be known to the world as Jello Biafra; a *nom de plume* chosen at random from a notebook after originally billing himself as Occupant.[3] "When I put the ads up I was dealing with different people," Ray continues. "Talking on the phone, then meeting with them and playing with them. I was working with someone else and Biafra at the same time, writing songs together. The other guy showed up an hour late. And that was it. I said, 'I've been waiting here an hour. Thank you very much. Bye.' They were both talented. But everyone in DKs had that craftsman work ethic, about showing up on time. This won't get anywhere [otherwise]. It's about commitment."

Biafra had grown up in Boulder, Colorado, the son of a librarian mother and a psychiatric social worker father who also wrote poetry. Both endorsed Martin Luther King's advocacy of passive resistance. Authority figures, notably a sixth-grade teacher who would daily profess what a good man Richard Nixon was, collided against an embryonic political consciousness forged by the anti-war demonstrations Eric could observe taking place at Colorado University from his elementary school window. As a consequence he immersed himself in the prevalent hippy culture, with its attendant stand against the Vietnam War and advocacy of environmentalism, civil rights and free love, but he later became horrified by its slide into exploitative practices and self-satisfaction. Realising how manipulative this community had become was fundamental to his worldview: "Seeing many hippies turn their backs on their ideals and evolve into what is now called New Age and Yuppies". He sought refuge instead in pranks and music. A shit-stirrer was born. Or rather, as Biafra prefers to have it, referencing Abbie Hoffman ('Sacred cows make the tastiest hamburgers'), the proud tradition of American shit-stirringdom had a new inductee.

While his family preferred classical music, the first records he possessed were by Creedence Clearwater Revival and Steppenwolf, Christmas gifts both, followed by a couple of Led Zeppelin albums and the *Woodstock* soundtrack. "Blue Öyster Cult are significant," he adds, "because their *Tyranny and Mutation* was the first one I ever bought without first hearing the songs on the radio. I was fed up with radio by age thirteen, in 1971, so I started buying records whose covers looked cool, especially since that first one really hit the spot. My big later interests also included The Stooges, Pink Fairies, 13th Floor Elevators, Hawkwind, Frank Zappa, Black Sabbath and, believe it or not, Sparks, because their lyrics and songs were so demented, especially the *Indiscreet* album."

Many of these initial purchases were through local store Trade-A-Tape, nearby his high school. Faithfully dedicated to servicing country-rock to local residents, the proprietors would throw anything they regarded as slightly weird into a free box outside the store. Later he was fortunate enough to discover the original Wax Trax store in Denver, run by Jim Nash and Dannie Flesher, who later moved the shop to Chicago and set up the famed record label of the same name. "All of a sudden, I noticed this window and it had old Yardbirds records in it, and a John Denver record nailed onto the door, nails through his eyes and blood pouring out . . . and I figured, aha, this is the place for me."

MC5 were also an important addition to his growing musical consciousness. "What got me clued into them was the music critic of *The Denver Post*. His name was Jared Johnson. He did capsule reviews of albums every week. Boy, did he go off on albums he didn't like. He said that Paul Simon and the Bee Gees were the greatest composers of the twentieth century, but he ranted and raved against Alice Cooper and said that Black Sabbath was almost as bad as MC5. So I immediately went out and started looking for MC5 albums the next day." He found two of them for 25 cents at Trade-A-Tape.

Despite a propensity for mentally warehousing large tracts of information and a fascination with printed and visual media (which would later manifest itself in the collage art that would accompany Dead Kennedys records) music singularly inspired Biafra's love of words. "Music lyrics are almost my entire literary background," he confirms. "This seems to shock and annoy a hell of a lot of people, although Allen Ginsberg thought it was great and perfectly valid. At the very least, it helps me overcome my intellectual upbringing to hopefully better communicate to other people raised on music lyrics who don't really like to read."

While still in Boulder he roadied for Colorado's first punk band, The Ravers. They would subsequently relocate to New York and eventually had a 1984 hit with '88 Lines About 44 Women' for RCA under new name, The Nails. Irony fans will note that the A&R link was Bruce Harris, the man credited with finally convincing Epic to release The Clash's debut album in America and invoking the epithet 'The only band that matters'. However, Biafra's first noteworthy musical venture was The Healers. They specialised in "real scary music" and did some tentative recording but never played live. "We never rehearsed," confirms Biafra, "it was me and John Greenway and sometimes others banging on instruments we couldn't play when our parents weren't home. It was all improvised."

Sensing the winds of change overseas, a trip to England in the summer of 1977 saw Biafra check out the local punk scene. He was able to attend shows by The Count Bishops and Little Bob Story, and caught an early Wire gig supporting The Saints (he was so impressed by the latter he had them sign a copy of *I'm Stranded*). On his return he enrolled at the University of California at Santa Cruz that autumn to study Drama and the History of Paraguay – simply because they were the only classes left on offer (he'd tried to get into film school but didn't make the cut). Inspired by repeat spins of the Sex Pistols' 'Anarchy In The UK' – he had been amongst the first residents of Boulder to possess a copy – he cut off his hippy hair, placed it inside a Ziploc bag and nailed the spurned locks to his dorm door. "That was just inspiration because I felt the hippy thing had run its course. They weren't causing enough of the right kind of trouble anymore. As soon as the hair went off, all of a sudden I felt dangerous again from the way people reacted. The bag of hair still exists! I've got it somewhere. I found it a while back!"

About ten weeks was all he could stomach in a campus environment of "pathetic Deadheads with rich parents". He dropped out before completing his first semester, returning to Boulder to subsist by washing soiled laundry at a nursing home, which presented his very own *One Flew Over The Cuckoo's Nest* moment. "A fascinating journey into hell", not least because he was appalled at the practices of some orderlies who traded in watches and other effects stolen from the unfortunate inmates.

When San Francisco became his final port of call he was primed to embrace the first West Coast American bands such as the Germs, Dils, Sleepers and particularly the Screamers. "When I moved back out, it took two days to get there. I happened to arrive on the night that The Nuns and Negative Trend were playing." Enthused, he put into action previously frustrated plans to start a new band by responding to Ray's advert. After all, one of the first people he'd met in San Francisco was Negative Trend's Will Shatter. "Hey, you should be in a band," he informed Biafra. "I've been playing bass for only three days and I'm in a band."

The next respondent, after Biafra and Ray had kicked the band idea around for a month or so, was Klaus Flouride, aka Geoffrey Lyall. Like Ray he was a time-served musician, having played in bands around New York and Boston for several years. In his native Detroit, he would regularly tape shows by some of that city's legendary performers. "I had actually recorded early on people like MC5, early Stooges etc. at the Grande Ballroom," he says. "They were fairly crude tapes, but pretty good." However, his entire cassette collection was stolen from his basement during a black-out. "I'm sure they took it to a pawn shop and the guy gave them four bucks for the whole thing. The tapes, whoever got them, they probably erased them and put their Fleetwood Mac collection on it. But I definitely got to see a lot of that stuff fairly close up. And got to examine it."

He was first drawn to music when his brother and sister started buying him records in the mid-'50s. "I saw Buddy Holly on TV. I saw Elvis on the *Ed Sullivan Show*. And I saw Jerry Lee Lewis and all that stuff. But it was Buddy Holly that made me ask my parents to get me a guitar for Christmas. I figured they'd get me a Stratocaster. That's what he was playing. And they got me this big old Stellar acoustic from Sears. And it had a neck on it like a horse's leg, and I was a little eight-year-old kid. And my fingers couldn't even fit around the neck. The guitar teacher got very frustrated, and told my parents I'd never play."

He started his own pirate radio station in Detroit before moving to Boston, where he studied communications. "I had pirate radio stations in Detroit in '65/'66, and in Boston from '71 to '74. In Detroit it was WKMA for 'Kiss My Ass'. Basically, we got bothered a whole bunch of times in Detroit, so we moved over to Canada, where the FCC [Federal Communications Commission] couldn't touch us, and the Canadian Board of Broadcasting didn't care one way or the other, because we weren't jamming anybody. And we'd get these letters entirely in red from the FCC. But we knew they couldn't do a thing. In Boston it was WOMB – the station with immaculate reception! I was on Beacon Hill, so I had good range up the Charles River – MIT [Massachusetts Institute of Technology], Harvard, Boston University; all those people on the river, in the dorms. When it started out in Detroit we were playing everything from Lenny Bruce to early Mothers to stuff like Iggy Pop. By the end of that station's existence we had some MC5 and stuff like that. It was before freeform radio really happened out here. The transmitter came because we knew this guy who was a science freak. And he said, 'Oh, I can build a transmitter.' And he did! The first one was a World War II field radio that had a monster tube in the middle of it. It was supposed to broadcast in the short wave area. He just knocked it down to the AM band. But we had to turn it off ten minutes in every hour because it would overheat. Then he built us a better one from scratch. Then when we moved to Canada he built a 1,000-watt transmitter. But I don't have that one. That was left in Detroit with one of the other guys who ran the station with me."

At the same time, he began playing in bands. "When I first started playing in Boston, it was cover bands. Then there was this guy Billy Squier, who played in Tom Swift And His Electric Grandma. He and I got together and had this group called Magic Terry & The Universe. It was inspired by things like MC5 and The Stooges and was involved in the Warhol scene. Terry was a very charismatic front-person who did not sing; he spoke everything. We had one gig, playing with Ten Years After. We were a Velvet Underground kind of group, and kids were there mostly to see a guy play very fast guitar. [Terry] had this song called 'Of America And The Entire Western World'. It was a seven-minute song he played eight different characters in. And towards the end of the set, Terry mooned the kids. We were supposed to be playing three or four days but got booted off after the first night. The story that came back to New York was 'banned in Boston' and everyone got excited. But then it fizzled out. Both the record companies that were excited about it said, 'We're not ready for you yet, we'll sign you in a year. Get the stuff together.' We couldn't hold out for a year. We were nineteen-year-olds and didn't want to wait that long." At one point Jim Morrison got Magic Terry a meeting with The Doors' management team, but Terry was considered, even by that interlocutor's standards, too volatile.

"When that broke up I started playing R&B and blues stuff. That's what basically I did for ten years, playing in house blues bands. When blues masters came through they'd use our bands. Albert Collins, John Lee Hooker – people like that would use us. Some people would practice, others would assume that we'd know their stuff. But we had our own side bands, R&B-type bands. And it would get to the point where it would be a bunch of white guys challenging black guys to see who could drink more. I got tired of that. So I decided to check out California to see if it was different. I came out to visit in the Christmas of '76." The temperature was in the high '70s. "A little drizzle, that's all. It turns out it was an incredible warm snap in San Francisco. I didn't know that. I thought, that's just what California is like. I went back to Boston and I was driving a cab at that point. We had some amazing snowstorms in Boston, which was really good for cabs because people would constantly flag you down from one stop to the next. You'd get ten bucks for taking someone half a mile. Then they'd tip you another three and there was someone else frantically flagging you down. So I made enough to buy a van and move out to San Francisco in May 1977."

It was while driving cabs he first heard about punk. "I got the first Ramones album for 50 cents. I took it home, played it and laughed at it. I thought it was kinda funny, but amateurish, and I pooh-poohed it. But then I woke up the next morning with those tunes still running through my head. And I thought, ah, that's curious, that it just needled its way into my brain that quickly. So I got to San Francisco. I was working as a temp, going out on Fridays for drinks with people. One of the places we'd go to was the Mabuhay. The first band I saw there that made an impression on me was The Zeros. They'd been based in San Diego and moved up to San Francisco. The people I was with were laughing at the whole thing, like – what a joke! I sat there thinking, this is intense. This is what rock 'n' roll used to be about when I was a kid. It was like Little Richard and Jerry Lee Lewis and all that stuff that scared my parents when we watched it on the *Ed Sullivan Show*. When Jerry Lee Lewis came on, my mother let out a sigh of relief, cos the guy looked like a classical musician sitting down at the piano. He sat down and then started playing. He plays a little wild, then he stood up and he threw his hair forward, and his whole hair comes flying out. My mom just said, 'Oh, my God!' I was just glued to the television. And that's the kind of thing that I would say punk rock was doing again, whereas anything else going on in rock 'n' roll in the mid to late '70s was *not* doing that."

Shortly afterwards he chanced across Ray's ad in *Bay Area Musician*. "BAM was a magazine to fill up the void so there was somebody to stroke bands on the local Jefferson Starship kind of level. It ignored punk. I was looking through the back of that and there was a guy looking to form a punk band. And it said 'East Bay – which was the part of the Bay Area that Ray lives in – Ray.' And because I'd only been in San Francisco for a while and wasn't familiar with the terms, I wasn't sure if his name was East Bay or Ray or East Bay Ray. So I played it safe and called him Ray when we spoke on the phone. I told him that story about a year later and that's when he settled on East Bay Ray. On the 'California Über Alles' single, he's Ray Valium."

He made his way over to Ray's garage for the first practice session. "The first thing he [Ray] asked was, 'Can you play "Peggy Sue"?' I had that one right down, it was one of the first things I learned on guitar. It was close to a regular punk progression.

Ray wanted to play something that had that kind of sound without being a Ramones song that you'd memorised – 'Let's not go to the garage and play 'Sheena Is A Punk Rocker'. Let's go to the garage and see if you can play the *roots* of 'Sheena Is A Punk Rocker''." I remember a phone conversation where I was mentioning The Residents and Devo influence. Most of the other people were just saying Sex Pistols and Ramones. It just showed that we had a drive to make it sound like something that would stand out and not just be generic-sounding."

And so began Dead Kennedys. Even today the sight of their name can send the uninitiated into a fit of apoplexy. It was chosen to symbolise "the end of the American dream and the beginning of the decline and fall of the American Empire," a myth most exquisitely enshrined in the fate of the Kennedy clan. To most Americans its invocation was, and remains, an act of sacrilege. Rather than playing to punk consensus, it was additionally a specific affront to the mainstream liberals of the Democratic Party. A good start then.

That moniker came from Biafra – in a roundabout way. Given that his ability to coin band names is legendary (documented on his *No More Cocoons* spoken word album), it is somewhat surprising that its original source was a third party. Or rather, perhaps, parties. "It was suggested by two friends at the same party," remembers Biafra, "one of whom was a guy called Rick Stott." Stott, later the DKs' lawyer, had worked the counter at Trade-A-Tape, managed The Ravers and would later join the staff at *Maximum Rock 'n' Roll* radio show, prior to its fanzine incarnation. "The other one was Radio Pete [aka Mark Bliesener, future *New York Rocker* contributor and editor of *Rocky Mountain Musical Express*, who subsequently managed Lyle Lovett, Alan Parsons and The Nitty Gritty Dirt Band]. The funny part is – only a few years ago did Rick Stott tell me that he suggested that as a great band name after reading about another band called Dead Kennedys in Cleveland! Then *our* Dead Kennedys starts. Ray Farrell, who later ran SST Records and was hired by Geffen, was working at a record store called Rather Ripped in Berkeley and said, 'Yeah, you guys are getting all this great press in Cleveland.' And I thought, 'What?' I picked up an issue of *Cle*, the fanzine that Pere Ubu and the rest were covered in, and looked at it and realised that it was a completely different band. Had I known that there was *another* band of that name already, I would never have used it." In fact, the Cleveland Dead Kennedys had swiftly changed their name after they discovered the name was something of an impediment to getting live bookings.

In fact, Bliesener has a much clearer recollection of the provenance of what Jon Savage would acknowledge as "the definitive punk name". "Rick actually came up

YOUNG *ERIC BOUCHER*, IMPRESSED BY THE ENERGY, POLITICS, AND CULTURAL TERRORISM OF THE PUNK SCENE, MOVES TO SAN FRANCISCO.

I WANT TO *DO* THIS!

WILL SHATTER

GREAT SHOW, SHATTER!

HEY-YOU SHOULD BE IN A BAND, ERIC! I'VE BEEN PLAYING BASS FOR ONLY THREE DAYS & I'M IN A BAND!

ON JUNE 5TH 1978, TEN YEARS FROM THE ASSASSINATION OF PRESIDENTIAL HOPEFUL ROBERT KENNEDY...

NAME: RAY GUITAR, 6 YRS. HAS FINANCIAL BACK WANTS LEAD SINGER, KEYBD, B OR A BAND F NEW WAVE PUNK.

THAT AD MAY BE JUST THE THING ...

I'M RAY GLASSER.

HI! I'M ERIC BOUCHER.

LIKE THE AD SAID, I'VE PLAYED GUITAR FOR 6 YEARS. I'D BEEN IN A BAND CALLED *CRUISIN'*. WE DID BEACH BOYS COVERS, BUT MAINLY WE PLAYED ROCKABILLY.

NOW, I WANT TO DO PUNK!

ME TOO! I LOVE THE SEX PISTOLS, THE DAMNED, AND THE STRANGLERS. DID YOU CATCH THE PISTOLS AT WINTERLAND?

I THOUGHT THE AVENGERS WERE GREAT!

3

I'M KLAUS FLUORIDE. I'M FROM DETROIT. GROSSE POINT, ACTUALLY. I WAS INTO FUNK. THAT'S WHAT GOT ME INTO PLAYING BASS.

I'M BRUCE SLESINGER. CALL ME TED. I'D BEEN INTO JAZZ, BUT...

WHAT ARE WE GONNA CALL OURSELVES?

HOW ABOUT DEAD KENNEDYS?

CESAR ROMERO FAN CLUB

IT'S A BIT MUCH!

NO GOOD. WE'LL NEVER GET SIGNED WITH THAT KIND OF NAME!

YEAH. WE DECIDED TO CALL OURSELVES THE DEAD KENNEDYS!

UH-HUH.

CALL ME 6025.

WE'VE GOT A GIG!

WE STILL NEED A NAME FOR THE BAND.

WELL I'VE ALREADY TOLD EVERYONE THAT WE'RE CALLING OURSELVES THE DEAD KENNEDYS.

HEH HEH, TOO LATE TO CHANGE IT NOW!

with Gang of Four – before there was a Gang of Four!" Bliesener recalls. [Gang of Four was actually a name coincidentally suggested by Biafra.] "I had been toting the name around to some other bands as well. Word had gotten around. In about 1974 I had moved from Chicago to a cabin with no water, and my girlfriend was staying with me and had a teddy bear she called 'Ted Kennedy', in honour of the senator. Just out of that came the notion one night when we were sitting around, 'Ted Kennedy – Ted Kennedy – *Dead* Kennedy'. What a great name for a band! It just kind of lay there. I have kept a running band name list forever. I've either been in or worked with bands my whole life. This just went on the list. Eventually I moved back to Colorado from Los Angeles, where I was playing with ? and the Mysterians. In 1976. In July, just after I'd moved in, I was doing some recording for fun, with the Dead Kennedys name in mind. I wrote a couple of songs, one was '(Just) A Patsy', after Lee Harvey Oswald's famous line, and another one, 'Jackie's Song'. I recorded those for the bicentennial in 1976.[4] At that time, everyone in Colorado who appreciated Mott, the Dolls, the Velvets, The Stooges, Phil Spector, Pistols, The Damned, The Clash – we all ran into one another. I had a PA system, which I hired out for like $50 a time. One was The Ravers [whose drummer, Al Leis, would later audition for the Dead Kennedys after Ted departed] and hanging around that band was Eric and a kid named Joseph Pope [later behind the *Rocky Mountain Low* compilation and bass player of SST band Angst]. I remember we were all so passionate, that feeling that if we didn't seize control and get some three-chord rock out there it would disappear and become a museum piece. I ended up going to Eric's parents' house to his boyhood bedroom and brought my cassette recorder – I was taping singles he'd brought back from the UK. We couldn't get them here yet; Cortinas, Vibrators, X-Ray Spex, I think. I was just taping off his record player, and probably preaching the gospel of Phil Spector. I recall saying to him, 'I have the greatest name for a band that nobody could *ever* use.' It just lay there. I was totally surprised when I heard about that first Dead Kennedys show in 1978. How cool! Someone actually used that name!"

Biafra had to employ a little subterfuge to get his own way, however. "When I suggested Dead Kennedys, Ray and Klaus objected so strongly I knew I was onto something. So I told The Dils, Negative Trend and others that Dead Kennedys was our name, and Ray and Klaus couldn't get rid of it!" They immediately started writing songs together, but their memories of the methodology vary wildly. "I had one

Previous spread: Pages from Dead Kennedys 'Hard Rock' comic, originally published by Revolutionary Comics. Reproduced by kind permission of Jay Allen Sanford of Rock 'n' Roll Comics. This issue, according to Sanford, was written "by a woman who at the time was a Sociology professor at DePaul University, where she used our comics in her courses!" Words by Deena Dasein, artwork by Joe Paradise.

of those $10 cassette recorders," Ray states. "Different songs were written different ways, but he [Biafra] would say his words into the cassette and I'd record them, and find some chord changes later, or something would happen right then. Then later I gave him cassettes with guitar riffs, melody lines and chords. He would rummage through his booklet of lyrics and find one that fit. Another way that songs would happen would be that we were jamming together and record it. Which is how 'Holiday In Cambodia' came about."

This is not how Biafra recollects the development of the songs at all, although 'Cambodia' is an exception. He is adamant that the concepts for the vast majority of songs were his, and they were not only lyrics, but came with his ideas on the riffs and music that should accompany them. "I never *once* handed Ray any lyrics to make into a song," he maintains. "The only time I ever did that with anybody was the one time with Carlos." Carlos Cadona, aka 6025, was the band's temporary second guitarist, whom everyone in the band seems to refer to affectionately as 'eccentric'. "I was hanging around with Carlos," Biafra continues, "and we both liked really weird music and were hot to be in a band. Then his band Mailman broke up. So I said, 'Why not just join our band?'" Ray remembers 6025 as someone they know from local shows. "He played guitar, so we started playing with him. He added that Captain Beefheart/Frank Zappa overtone to things."

Biafra didn't, at this stage, have much in the bank in the way of lyrics. "I actually had very little. I was new to the whole thing. It sort of occurred to me late in the game that if I was going to be in a band, it would help to have songs. If I wanted good lyrics, I was going to have to write them myself. It became a case of trial and error. At first it was mainly me walking in with complete songs – I'd play them single-string on a guitar to show them to Ray – then later Ray brought in one of his own, 'Your Emotions'. The very first time I met Ray, I went over there with my guitar, and showed him the song that became 'Kepone Factory' [later released on *In God We Trust, Inc.*], originally called 'Kepone Kids'. Originally it was the more clichéd title, 'Kepone Kids'. The second one I brought in was a song we never released, called 'Kidnap.'" The latter concerned the case of Patty Hearst, who served time for aiding and abetting her kidnappers, self-styled left-wing guerrillas the SLA, in an armed robbery. "The lyrics were printed in *Search And Destroy*, but we didn't save the song and put it on *Fresh Fruit*. I think I wrote that after I got to San Francisco. The third song was 'California Über Alles'. That was one of the few that, rather than have the music in my head, I actually blundered into the verse-riff while playing around with my room-mate's bass one night. The other parts came later." The original draft of 'California' had been written with old Boulder friend John Greenway, who actually performed the song alongside Biafra as part of The Healers. Greenway wrote the words after listening (voluntarily or otherwise) to Biafra's discourse on state governor Jerry Brown.[5] The chorus, with Biafra's distinctive vibrato/warble, once dubbed a 'human theremin', was inspired by Japanese Kabuki music. "Although the timing of the chorus seemed perfectly logical to me, it took the other guys a month to get the timing right. It's not in any conventional sheet music timing or anything. I don't worry about that, I just make the stuff up."

Ray is pretty animated in disputing this. "Here's the problem: when there's stuff that I do, it's always *the band*. When there's stuff that Biafra does, it's always *himself*. That's how Biafra spins things. He won't give credit to anybody else in the band. Everybody in the band was like that, I feel – we all worked to make the songs as good as possible. The problem is that he says this, this and this. And the other people, if they don't put something equally in, it looks like he's doing it all. Biafra's much more comfortable talking about himself than Klaus or myself are. We're much more laidback, low-key people. He's a lead singer! Lead singers speak in 'I' a lot. Klaus really was instrumental in the songwriting, but he won't take credit for it. Every time Biafra says 'his', Klaus and I is what he's talking about. I have a balance issue on that one . . . because we all really worked to make the songs."

Biafra insists that beyond these early efforts, he never had a booklet of lyrics to rummage through. "To this day, I never finish anything unless I'm going to use it. There were cassettes with his riffs on it that he [Ray] gave me later. Those riffs are sprinkled into the songs on [subsequent Dead Kennedys albums] *Plastic Surgery Disasters* and *Frankenchrist*. A little bit on *Bedtime For Democracy*. They are all credited accordingly. At least they were before they lied and changed all the songwriting credits. But *Fresh Fruit*, the original credits, most of the songs were written by me. If I hadn't brought them in, arranged and all, they would not exist. They did not dispute those original credits for twenty years."

What all those early songs did have, right from the outset, was lashings of sarcasm. "I think humour can be a powerful weapon. Why else was Charlie Chaplin run out of the United States during the Red Scare and McCarthy era?"

New WAVE concert

Young ADULTS

avengers

sudden Fun

Dead Kennedys

$3

ALTOS

1920 san pablo (corner hearst)

sat oct 28

ten pm

From L.A.
ALLEY CATS & BAGS

DEAD KENNEDYS

SAT. OCT. 6
1839 GEARY

SAN FRANCISCO
924-6032

AVENGERS
DEAD KENNEDYS
MUTANTS
SATURDAY
DEC. 16
9:30
AT
330 GROVE
ADMISSION:
3 BUCKS.
Poster by ALTERNATIVE TENTACLES

Join the people who've joined the Army.

Chapter 2

In a Desperate Mind,
Little Gardens Grow

Shut Up You Animals
Dirk Dirksen (1937–2006), ringmaster of the circus of the creatively inspired and
willfully deranged, presided as Pope of Punk over nightly excursions into living
theater on the premises 1974–1984 at Ness Aquino's Mabuhay Gardens, previously
a Filipino supper club. He opened the lid on society's garbage can of new talent to look
for truth and beauty that gave rise to San Francisco's counter-culture music scene.
(Plaque commemorating Dirk Dirksen)

Say goodnight, Dirk! You can say what you want, but how many people
have been willing to put up with you, and us, for seven or eight years?
(On-stage dedication by Biafra to Dirksen, recorded on the introduction
to 'Police Truck' on the bootleg *Never Been On MTV*)

ead Kennedys made their live debut on a bill headed by The Offs at Ness Aquino's Mabuhay Gardens. Sandwiched between a row of strip joints and booked by Dirk Dirksen, the venue is held in similar esteem to New York's CBGB's, London's Roxy and LA's Masque as one of the key formative locales in punk history.

"If you were in a band in 1975 or 1976," Jeff Raphael of The Nuns would tell James Stark in his book *Punk '77*, "you had to be in what the 'local scene' was at that time or there was nowhere to play. That's why we started the Mabuhay. There was nowhere for anybody to go. We had to create our own place to hang out, so that's what we did. Before Mabuhay, I never hung out in clubs because there wasn't a club scene. With the Mabuhay, you just went there. You didn't care who was playing, because you went to hang out."

Dirksen, a former tour manager for Ray Charles and The Doors, was renowned for baiting his audiences to 'amp' gigs prior to performance, his faithful pooch

Above left: Mutants play Napa State Mental Hospital 1978. Left to right: Brendan, Sue, Fritz, Sally, Charlie and John Mutant. (Photograph by Ruby Ray)
Below left: *Search And Destroy* Headquarters 1977. Vale's apartment in North Beach. (Photograph by Ruby Ray)

Dummy tucked under his arm as he traded insults with bands. He claimed to have had his nose broken several times as a result and in one incident Michael Kowalski, 'mentor' of U.X.A., smashed his cash register and snapped his glasses. Dirksen eventually let him back in the club after U.X.A. singer and girlfriend De De Droit negotiated a deal whereby the cost of his glasses would be recouped from Kowalski's social security cheque. "Dirk told me he insulted all the bands as a way of treating everyone equally and not playing favourites," Biafra confirms, who also credits him with being the impetus behind all-ages shows. "I was never carded when I went to punk shows in London as a nineteen-year-old in '77. The key in San Francisco was Dirk. All Mabuhay shows were all-ages." As a consequence an atmosphere some-where between camaraderie and confrontation prevailed at the 'Fab Mab'.

"They had a meeting every month where representatives of each band were supposed to go down and dicker with Dirk Dirksen about who wanted a gig," recalls Biafra, "who could play with whom, etc. It was more of a free-for-all than negotiation. I was a pretty low man on the totem pole, because we'd never played and no-one had actually seen us. I was already a known guy on the scene, though. I pogo-danced a little wilder than most, which annoyed some people, but . . . Sometimes I would jump off the front of the stage while another band was playing. Not a true stage dive, cos the stage wasn't high enough. Part of what drew people to see us the first time was – oh, *this guy* has a band now. Let's see what this is!" A view confirmed by local photographer Ruby Ray. "I do remember that we were all wondering what Biafra would do as we (the other hardcore) had seen him around at all the shows. He did sleep on our living room floor for a few months when he ran for mayor."

Biafra as the local nutter? "Yeah. Considered the local nutter, especially by The Dils and The Nuns. Unfortunately, two important bands broke up right before we debuted. So it was fortunate for us, but not for a very good reason, because we'd lost The Sleepers, one of my all-time favourite bands, as well as U.X.A. So people were hungry for a new band. Plus, the scene was thriving but quite small, so people would get bored if they saw the same band with everybody they knew in them time after time and nobody came up with anything new. What especially made it different from later punk underground scenes, and especially the above ground scenes of today; the pressure was not on every band to sound the same and please the audience and cater to their expectations. The pressure was on every band to sound different, to offer something fresh. If you completely fucked with people, *Metallic KO* or Negative Trend-style, so much the better."

Dirksen requested a bio and a glossy photo. "Since at the time we didn't have a drummer," Biafra continues, "we borrowed Carlos and he posed as the drummer." To this day, Carlos/6025 is routinely credited as the band's first percussionist, doubtless due to that first promotional photograph. "Dirk Dirksen did all the booking and promotion at the club," explains Ray. "He made it what it was. He said he needed an 8 x 10 glossy. He was trying to train us a bit on the business side of the music biz."

"All Dirk would hand me was a gig opening for an eccentric metal band," Biafra continues, "Magister Ludi, and a poppy new wave band, the Beans. Carlos and I were shaking our heads over that one. 'Oh, shit, we all have to start somewhere, but why *this*?' So I went back to Billy Hawk [guitarist] of The Offs and begged him to give us a better show. And so he put us on one of The Offs' shows as a fourth band. Usually there were only three. But that was a much better slot because it was us, and Negative Trend, and another band called DV8 before The Offs played. The Offs rescued us from probably having to battle another six months to get seen by the right people."

They'd already tried out various drummers, including one, the pseudonymous Rol Numb, who appeared on the practice tape that Ray recorded in order to secure the Mabuhay gig. "We had one drummer that came dressed in a bondage harness," Ray recalls. Presumably he'd read about UK punk fashion. "No, he might have actually been into it! He had really long hair, but he had this 'special' water. He was kind of an organic bondage dude." Biafra can't recall anyone auditioning in bondage harness, "but the long-haired guy [Rol Gjano aka Gene 'Geno' Rhymer] had a swastika pendant. The trivia part is that he played in a band before called Loose Gravel. They have a bit of a name because it was the band Mike Wilhelm did after The Charlatans, before he joined the Flamin' Groovies. Then he later called up Ray and complained about me, wanting Ray to kick me out because he thought I was a redneck! The sad part is, he was a really good drummer. But he really didn't get us. Never saw him in another band."

With the search becoming more frantic, enter Ted, aka Bruce Slesinger, a graduate of New York's Pratt Institute of Architecture and the final piece in the jigsaw. "I'd just moved out here from the east." Ted recalls. "I had a job here working in an architect's office, just doing drafting and that sort of thing. I came to San Francisco and put my name up on a bulletin board looking for other musicians. I get a call from Klaus. Was I interested in joining Dead Kennedys, or at least coming round for a try-out? Since I hadn't heard from anybody else, I said OK."

Like the other musicians in the band, Ted brought experience to bear. "I first started playing drums when I was around twelve. I would play in the band and the school orchestra. Then my parents bought me a used drum set. I played that for a while and really got into it. Then I started playing with friends. I played once in the Café Wha? in New York, which was a club in the Village. I wasn't serious about it when I was fourteen or fifteen. It was just fun with friends, that's all."

He'd actually spotted Ray's ad previously in Aquarius Records, but passed. "Yeah, the ad said 'Dead Kennedys – looking for drummer'. It was in a local record store. I saw this name and thought, I'm not going to call them with *that* name. Then I put my own ad up. Then Klaus called me! It turned out better. At that time there were a lot of really terrible bands, people looking to play with other musicians. A lot of people were just starting up. Anyone who could play two chords was trying to form a band at the time. I was pleasantly surprised when I got to their audition and I thought Ray and Klaus were great musicians."

The appreciation was mutual. "He was the first person who rushed us on one of the songs," says Klaus, "everyone else was dragging. Bruce actually rushed us ahead of the beat. So I just handed him a beer and said, 'Do you wanna be in the group?' And he said sure, and that was that. So then we practised five days a week or something to get ready for that show." Ted's recall of that first meeting is similar. "I think it was at Ray's house, the first audition. They said to me afterwards, 'You're the first drummer who can keep up with us. Are you interested in playing next week? We have a gig.'" What did Ted make of the songs? "They just seemed very quick. They were decent enough, and it was fun just to play." Ray's primary emotion was relief. "Bruce only joined a week before the show. But luckily, he's a very talented drummer! We were auditioning different drummers in my garage. I still only live a block from where it all started. The garage has been torn down unfortunately. So we rehearsed there, but once we got a drummer the neighbours started noticing. We had to move." Carlos, aka 6025, had been inducted into the band just before, as a guitarist, and had the same five days' grace prior to their live debut.

Dead Kennedys duly made their debut at Mabuhay Gardens on 19 July 1978. With the growing popularity of the 'Fab Mab', San Francisco had its first settled venue for punk acts. A big part of the reason was because its food licence allowed under-21s to attend. It worked something like this; the venue was indeed a restaurant until about 11pm, at which time the patrons would be kicked out and a very different crowd ushered in. Three hours of music and drinking would ensue. "The reason punk scenes didn't start as early in a lot of American cities," notes Biafra, "is because there weren't all-ages venues. So it was more like a bar band playing Fleetwood Mac covers, four sets a night, for the burnt-out adults. That was all local music was allowed to be. Including in my hometown, where it was country-rock instead, and everyone wanted to be the next Eagles."

The show proved to all concerned that they were on to something. "It [the Mabuhay] was as big as you could get in San Francisco," recalls Ray, "because Blondie had played there back in the day, stuff like that. The thing I remember is that we didn't have a complete set, we had a 20-minute set. But we were so excited we played that 20-minute set in 15 minutes!" Klaus, too, was blown away. "We even got an encore as an opening band and there were a lot of other bands on the bill. So we had to go out and repeat 'Rawhide' or something like that, because we didn't have anything else." Biafra reckons the set was over in just 11 minutes, and the encore was 'Man With The Dogs', which hadn't been part of the main set. "It was really wild, a lot of fun," enthuses Ted. "We immediately got a great reception. It was very encouraging and we got a high coming off stage. We did play real fast and we got a great response. The band just immediately took off from that point, it was pretty exciting."

They played regularly thereafter in San Francisco, though the notoriety of their name necessitated some variance in billing; The Creamsicles and Pink Twinkies were two flags of convenience, though, contrary to reports elsewhere, they were never known as The Sharks. "They were used once each to play high school dances incognito," Biafra recalls. "First one worked, second one didn't. The Sharks was what Ray wanted to call the band itself!" The aforementioned Creamsicles show, organised at Moraga High School as a Christmas dance under the flag of the Whittler's Club, a sanctioned but inactive fraternity, ended up as a sneak punk rock bill with Sudden Fun and The Zeros supporting. "The image that remains," stated John Marr later of *Maximum Rock 'n' Roll* in San Francisco punk oral history *Gimme Something Better*, "is the band playing their music while Biafra is being dragged around in the back of the cafeteria. It was great fun."

Their third show at the Mabuhay resulted in a mass of broken furniture and a lecture from Dirksen about 'violating the theatre of illusion'. At a show at Project One (aka The Pit) the hippy commune living there objected to the audience who turned out to see the DKs, Mutants and KGB. Promoter Paul 'Rat' Bakovich would subsequently move his operations to 330 Grove Street and continue; but The Pit gig is notable for hosting the first public enactment of 'The Biafra'. Anyone who has seen the vocalist live will know he likes to 'act out' his creations; physically inhabiting the personas of power-drunk preachers, corrupt businessmen and politicians. 'The Biafra' saw audience members clamber on stage and attempt to imitate same, like a rowdy, tongue-in-cheek chorus line.

The name inevitably continued to cause complications. Among those to balk at their disrespect for America's leading family was Pulitzer Prize-winning news columnist Herb Caen. In 1978 he wrote in the *San Francisco Chronicle*: "Just when you think tastelessness has reached its nadir, along comes a punk rock group called The Dead Kennedys, which will play at Mabuhay Gardens on November 22, the fifteenth anniversary of John F. Kennedy's assassination. Despite mounting protests, the owner of Mabuhay says 'I can't cancel them NOW – there's a contract.' Not, apparently, the kind of contract some people have in mind." Of course, not for the last time in the band's history, the hysterics of the press simply furthered their cause. The Mabuhay received several bomb threats and there was a fire truck stationed ominously outside on the night – but the venue was packed. As Biafra put it, "Every weird mind around crawled out of the woodwork to see us."

The reality was that Dirksen *did* originally cancel the band, but only in order to book a show by jazz legends Sun Ra. "But then Herb Caen complained, so he had to bring us back!" chortles Biafra. "Sun Ra played first, then the door charge was dropped and we played. The reaction of the black Muslims from the Sun Ra audience in their bow ties trying to flee the room as fast as possible was priceless. Sun Ra liked us, though!"

Search And Destroy was the estimable San Franciscan punk digest founded by V. Vale, who had formerly worked alongside poet Lawrence Ferlinghetti at the City Lights bookshop – the model on which Geoff Travis founded Rough Trade in the UK. When he announced his decision to start a punk fanzine in Christmas 1976, both Ferlinghetti and Allen Ginsberg helped out with finance. *Search And Destroy* ran the first major profile of the band in September 1978, under a fake *San Francisco Chronicle* strap-line. Alongside lyrics and photos of the original five-piece line-up, the group presented a list of influences including The Stooges, Silver Apples, Mick Farren, Hawkwind, Beefheart, Red Krayola and John Cooper Clarke, as well as contemporary peers F-Word, The Deadbeats and Half Japanese. In the interview Biafra set an admirable precedent by addressing any number of political topics with band promotion lagging a poor second.

Dead Kennedys' first recording sessions were undertaken at San Francisco's long established Different Fur Studios under the sponsorship of Bruce Conner, a respected artist from the beat era who also took photos for *Search And Destroy*. His

Above right: Gladhand, 1978. Biafra often acted like a politician, the audience's reaction was paramount. (Photograph by Ruby Ray)
Below right: The Girls' Bathroom at the Mab, 1978. Sally Webster from the Mutants, and everyone hung out there. (Photograph by Ruby Ray)

37

KENNEDYS
PLUS THE DEAD
AND DV 8
WITH NEGATIVE TREND
m. ranger '78

MILLER PRODUCTION
A DIRKSEN
THE OFFS
WEDNESDAY
JULY 19
MABUHAY Gardens
443 BROADWAY

38

1965 art film, *Report*, featured recurring footage of JFK's motorcade and had been played, without the band's consent, as the backdrop to their Mabuhay Gardens show on the anniversary of his assassination. "All of a sudden he wanted to be a producer," Ted remembers. "He paid for some sessions that we did at this very good recording studio called Different Fur. Between Biafra and Bruce, they never really saw eye to eye. It was slightly over-produced and didn't really capture the essence of the band, and the recording went nowhere." According to Klaus, the results were "incredibly slow versions, in retrospect". Biafra adds: "Yeah, they were slower, hardcore hadn't hit yet. I listened to them a few years later, and I thought they were cool. They reminded me of Joy Division."

"It was a dream came true that fell out of the sky," laments Biafra, "but turned out to be not what we thought it would be. Bruce Conner decided he wanted to start producing bands. And he picked us and got a deal where he'd trade art to [studio owner and electronic musician] Patrick Gleason of Different Fur in exchange for giving studio time. We thought things were sounding pretty good. But then Conner did a very different mix of 'California Über Alles' while we weren't there that sounds far more like Devo than Dead Kennedys. We didn't like that. He said it was a producer's right to interpret a band any way he wishes. We didn't agree, so then he got all mad at our mix, and said he wouldn't let any of the stuff come out." To this day it still hasn't.

Bootlegs confirm that at this stage Dead Kennedys' repertoire lacked the bite, spite and particularly the pace of the finished models. But illicitly circulated tapes of the band's demos offer worthy investigations into the development of the song cycle that led to *Fresh Fruit*. The origin of those recordings has long been held a mystery, though Ray has a theory that the source may be a recording studio that was next door to a rehearsal room they used. Biafra isn't having that. "Why does Ray make up these stupid stories? He recorded the '78 Demos himself on a high-quality cassette machine in March '79! We called it 'Carlos's Last Stand' because it was his last practice before he left the band and we wanted to get everything we knew on tape for posterity. Then we played the Deaf Club gig and he was gone."

Certainly sound quality would indicate, as opposed to the Different Fur recordings, that the '78 Demos were rehearsal sessions never intended for public scrutiny. And yet they offer up a series of clues and footnotes. 'Forward to Death' features an almost conventional rock guitar solo at its close. 'California Über Alles' is structurally similar to the familiar version though, as on the take of 'Kill The Poor', the vocals sound as if Biafra is on the verge of a hernia. While 'Your Emotions' features an extended outro, the 'effects damage' that turned up on the intro to the album version of

'Holiday In Cambodia' is present, if lacking in the sullen menace. On this and several other takes the vocals are almost whispered or talk-sung rather than employing the stridency one usually equates with Biafra. The lyrics on 'Cambodia' are different, too; the section of the couplet 'bragging that you know how the niggers feel cold' is herein swapped for a less visceral, less contentious, 'blacks' (live bootlegs confirm that this was the preferred vernacular at early shows). There are also slightly altered lyrics to 'I Kill Children', though it's the one song, alongside the cover of 'Viva Las Vegas', that comes close to replicating the urgency of its *Fresh Fruit* incarnation.

Of the unreleased songs, 'B-Flag' (as it is mistakenly labelled) is an early version of 'Kepone Factory'. 'Take Down' offers a standard punk riff with Biafra conducting as deranged cheerleader, while 'Cold Fish' is the nearest the band would come to straight Ramones pastiche (by way of Johnny Moped). But the real surprises are 'Undercover', aka 'Dreadlocks Of The Suburbs', a tongue-in-cheek flirtation with reggae, and a weird, loopy, avant-jazz instrumental, 'Psychopath', which reveals, and revels in, 6025's debt to Beefheart. "'Psychopath' is actually 'Mexican Monster Babies', states Biafra. "Which is also a Healers song. I pulled it after Carlos quit and John Greenway asked me not to use any more Healers songs. So I didn't."

However, Carlos's time with the band was coming to an end. He would leave after a final show at the Deaf Club on 3 March 1979 (the set was retrospectively released in 2004 as *Live At The Deaf Club*). He would return to play a guest role on *Fresh Fruit*.

Above right: Flyer for Dead Kennedys at the Deaf Club, 3 March 1979.
Below right: Flyer for Dead Kennedys, Controllers and Young Adults, Saturday 25 November 1979 at Aitos, Berkeley CA.
Overleaf pages 42-43: Portions of the collage poster given away with *Fresh Fruit For Rotting Vegetables*, designed by Jello Biafra.

Talking about... the dead kennedys ...

DEAD KENNEDYS DEAD KENNEDYS • • • • DEAD KENNEDYS DEAD KENNEDYS DEAD KENNEDYS

------plus several support bands----------

AT the DEAF CluB 530 VALENCIA St. S.F.

--------------MARCH 3, 1979 SATURDAY ----- 10:00 pm---- about 3.00 $

1 block from the
16th & Mission BART station

happy families   Plead Innocent

dead kennedys
controllers
YOUNG ADULTS

saturday
nov 25 9:30 p.m.

AITOS
1920 san pablo (corner hearst)
3 bucks

new wave hits berkeley!!
call 654 8768 for info
sound by third ear
video by target
minors o.k.

EXON

T YOU
ECT MY
ORPORATE
REST$!*

The red cross with its Muslim and Iranian alternatives

Hordes of the filthy
dents, some of them
inches long and the s
type that carried bu
plague in Europe d
the Middle Ages, swa
out of an excavatio
day and attacked pe
ans and cars, police

A woman pedestr
bitten as several of
mals reportedly
themselves aroun
and nibbled at he
witness said he s
stream down the
leg as she screar

Another passe
saw dozens of
jump onto a ca
at the windshi
and the car's vi

to swap bottles for candy

BA
SLA

From the Three

Merry
Christmas

Merry
Christmas

Merry
Christmas

THE ALFERD PACKER
MEMORIAL GRILL
Bottled 18

Chapter 3
You Will Jog for the Master Race

California is a queer place – in a way, it has turned its back on the world,
and looks into the void Pacific.
It is absolutely selfish, very empty, but not false,
and at least, not full of false effort.
(D.H. Lawrence)

fter the frustrations of the Different Fur sessions, the band repaired to a local studio to prepare its debut single. The key problem was the means of distribution. There were few A&R men falling over themselves to sign a band of their type, never mind one with such a cultural hand grenade of a name. "There weren't any deals to be had," relates Biafra. "The major labels had pulled the plug on their relationship with punk in early 1978, breaking the hearts of many of the key bands at the time who thought they were going to be signed. Everybody from the Weirdos and Screamers in LA to the Avengers, Nuns, Crime, Dils etc. in San Francisco." In fact, the odd unconsummated dalliance aside, no major label obliged an American punk band's dance card between The Dickies in 1978 (A&M) and Hüsker Dü (Warners) in 1985; and even then, only after Hüsker Dü's sound had changed substantially. Punk was 'over', apparently, though no-one had told Dead Kennedys, or more particularly, Biafra. "It wasn't over. It was one of those times that hits any musician every once in a while. You either play because you like to play, or you don't play at all. You don't play to get signed. You don't play to get big or famous, you play because you want to play. When I moved out to San Francisco, my goal was, as a record collector, to get my name on one 7-inch single. And be able to tell my grandkids I actually saw bands like The Dils and the Avengers and the Ramones in clubs before they were playing stadiums."

The band responded by setting up its own label, under the now familiar name Alternative Tentacles. There were few other options – contrary to some reports, there were no expressions of interest from major labels in the band until *Fresh Fruit* had sold so well in Britain. By this time the independent scene in the UK was well established, with Rough Trade, Chiswick, Beggars Banquet and others leading the charge – but that was not the case in America. The first punk-era independent in

San Francisco had opened. But Aquarius owner Chris Knab and promoter Howie Klein's 415 Records had financial ties to promoter Bill Graham, almost universally despised by punks, which would soon be co-opted by Columbia in any case. After initial releases by The Nuns and Mutants, it turned away from punk to concentrate on 'new wave' acts, notably Romeo Void. "Howie Klein, with Sire Records, he's the one promoting new wave/skinny tie bands," remembers Ray. "But he was anti-punk. And he was against us at the beginning. He wanted to promote the skinny tie/'My Sharona'-type band and bands like Blondie. Don't get me wrong, Blondie were a great band. I'm not saying new wave is bad. But Howie Klein thought punk would never go anywhere in the States, and we need to promote new wave. Now, he acts like he was there helping us out all the time – oh, the hypocrisy! But he was telling us to tone our music down and make it more new wave. Now, he's saying, he was there, supporting us 100%." Biafra has a more charitable view of Klein. "He did not hate punk, he was desperate to find his own Clash. But The Dils rejected him so he settled for the Red Rockers. Industry guy, yes, but it was he who got Sire to release [Ice-T's rap-metal fusion act] Body Count's 'Cop Killer' and got Warners to let Ministry make *Land Of Rape And Honey*. He is also one of the few industry insiders to publicly picket [former Washington wife and censorship campaigner] Tipper Gore. He's still an activist."

Subterranean Records, started by Mike Fox and Steve Tupper, would subsequently help fill the void and specifically gave licence to San Franciscan punk bands. But a whole swathe of great music was lost in the interim. "How I wish I could have had a label two years earlier," Biafra laments, "and put out all the great albums waiting to happen in the San Francisco area. The Avengers could have made at least three, and my favourite band of all, the Screamers [based in Los Angeles], never even made a record at all!"

'California Über Alles' was released in June 1979 and was an entirely home-spun creation. "We did the 'California Über Alles' single by ourselves," Ray recalls. "I remember shipping it off to Texas and having it shipped back to our house. Ted [who designed the original cover] and I sold it out of the back of our cars." After selling out of initial quantities, it was re-released by Optional. 'California Über Alles' was framed around the spectre of Governor Jerry Brown's ascent. Brown was an ambitious politician with an ostensibly left-leaning agenda, including advocacy of 'Buddhist economics'. Biafra originally considered him as dangerous as Nixon, "only less likely to make dumb mistakes". The song's lyric 'Big bro' on white horse is near' was paraphrased directly from one of his speeches: 'What the American people are looking for is a man on a big white horse.' Which made a good fit with the song's self-evident Orwellian references (and, in retrospect, with the punk community's anguish over the major label versus independent issue). Revealingly, Brown's early career was sponsored by David Geffen, the man whose company benefited most from Nirvana and the 'second-coming' of punk in the '90s. Brown also had a very public dalliance with Linda Ronstadt. The Eagles, Jane Fonda (later referenced in 'Kill The Poor') and Francis Ford Coppola numbered among Brown's supporters.

Other references to 'Zen fascists' in the song recall Biafra's adolescence in Boulder where the idealism of the '60s retreated to the greed of the '70s, garbed in fake hippy mysticism. In essence, it's a spiritual heir to Zappa's 'Who Needs The Peace Corps' from *We're Only In It For The Money*, the song that ridiculed San Francisco's Haight-Ashbury hippies. There's also a nod to Ingmar Bergman's 1977 Nazi-themed film *The Serpent's Egg* (itself a reference to a Brutus quote in Shakespeare's *Julius Caesar* concerning the emperor). The b-side, 'Man With The Dogs', profiled another character from Boulder, whose daily routine consisted of freaking out the town's residents by stopping and staring deep into their eyes – exactly the type of 'vacant stranger' who customarily fascinated Biafra. (5) The ending of 'Man With The Dogs', a kind of bespoke '60s garage psych with Ray's Echoplex skewering a repeated chord phrase into sonic oblivion, was an early indication that the band were not going to limit themselves to four-four punk.

Jerry Brown's politics would, perversely, eventually move closer to Biafra's own. "Jim Carroll [the late former punk musician and author of *The Basketball Diaries*] told me he'd spotted Brown at the Savoy Café in North Beach, and ran across the street to Recycle Records and bought the single and gave it to him, while he was governor," Biafra recalls. "We didn't hear anything from that. Many years later, Brown had veered very, very sharply to the left and beyond, and we were both working with Earth First. I encountered [film-maker] Michael Moore at a speaking engagement in San Francisco. We all went over to an Oakland warehouse space where Jerry Brown's people were serving a big dinner for everybody. One of the people working with Jerry who lived at his place came down and said – 'Oh, yeah, Jerry, this is Jello! I played Jerry your song this morning!' I have no idea what shade of red my face turned! He seemed more or less understanding."

For Ted, they never surpassed the original 'California Über Alles'. "That, to me, was the greatest. It was a great recording. It was much rawer than the Different Fur sessions. I think that track still sounds better than the one that's on *Fresh Fruit*. It was just a local recording studio, in the basement of Jim Keylor's house in San

Francisco." Keylor, a much-liked San Francisco musician who had previously played in Blue Cheer precursors The Oxford Circle, was in the process of establishing his Army Street Studios, which for some time would become a fixture of the local music community. "He was the engineer along with Ray, I guess," Ted continues. "But the sound was great. It was exciting. I found it had a lot more punch than the version we finally did on *Fresh Fruit*. The drumming was a little bit more unique, in part because the song had sped up so much from when we first did it till we finally did it for *Fresh Fruit*. By that time, it was difficult to do all those parts at twice the pace."

Biafra, who once had the stated ambition of collecting every punk record ever made, had been won over by an early UK obscurity by The Users, 'Sick Of You', housed on Cambridge's Raw Records imprint. He went to the trouble of bringing the single into the studio to show Jim Keylor the sound he wanted to achieve in the final mix, "but Ray's guitar setting was so different, we didn't have a chance". He agrees with Ted, however, on the primacy of that take of the song. "Yeah, I think the single versions of all our songs are better than the album versions. But I noticed that with other albums of the time, that the album version of the song rarely sounds as good as the single. The first time you record a song, especially if you've never recorded before, you're giving it everything you've got. And Jim Keylor went the extra mile to make it a good-sounding record. And re-recording 'California Über Alles' and 'Holiday In Cambodia' was kind of a drag. 'Wait a minute, we've done this already!'"

Of all the DKs back-catalogue, 'California Über Alles' has enjoyed the most intriguing afterlife, partly because Biafra has continually updated it.[6] Within a year of *Fresh Fruit*'s release it had become 'We've Got A Bigger Problem Now' on *In God We Trust, Inc.*, reflecting the election of Ronald Reagan as president. "That was just a result of the band goofing off at practice and at sound-check," notes Biafra. "Will Shatter from Flipper, who was one of our harshest critics – and one of *everybody*'s harshest critics! – he said, 'you're always so stiff, playing the same way – why don't you play it *that* way?' So it just wound up becoming an alternate version."

Given that California has seen fit to elect an increasingly surreal roll call of governors, it is no surprise that the investiture of Arnie Schwarzenegger in 2003 gave Biafra ammunition to revise the lyric once again. It would be re-imagined as 'Kali-Fornia Über Alles 21st Century' with both the Melvins (a live version was included on their second collaboration with Biafra, 2006's *Sieg Howdy*) and his current band, the Guantanamo School of Medicine. That he is able therein to incorporate an approximation of the Austrian's Comedy-Kraut accent provides too delicious an irony to forgo.

The phrase itself has now slipped into common parlance. The American-German author Gero Hoschek wrote a (so far unfilmed, though Biafra gave his blessing) screenplay with the title after titling his *Zeit* magazine article on the Golden State in its honour. Then there was the bizarre episode in 2010 when a right-wing commentator mischievously (we have to assume, no-one being *that* stupid) insisted that 'California Über Alles' was the perfect theme song for the Meg Whitman Republican campaign, in which she faced down and lost to our old friend Jerry Brown. "The very first single the band released in 1979 will make any California conservative's heart sing, I assure you," gushed Chip Hanlon. The calculated shit-storm that ensued ensured that Ray would appear on his radio show to put the record straight.

The band continued to play live wherever they could. Their first expeditionary tour of the East Coast was an unheard of venture for a Californian punk band, including a particularly memorable set at the Rat in Boston. "First the beer pitchers and trays flew," Biafra recalls. "Then the furniture flew. When we came back for our second set, everyone backed up, standing against the walls. The only band I'd ever heard of that got a reaction like that was The Stooges. So I was very proud that evening – one of my all-time favourite gigs. 'Welcome to the West Coast, motherfuckers!'" The story about him being beat up by an indignant waitress included on the 25th anniversary DVD of *Fresh Fruit* is, unfortunately, untrue. "She scratched my chest – big deal – then fled the room."

They also played Max's Kansas City in New York opening for the Voodoo Shoes, a singularly inappropriate billing. "That tour was a drag," Biafra laments, "because it wasn't all-ages in the US north-east. It was a horrible bar band scene with tables and chairs. Maybe someone would get up and dance with their date and . . . Yecch! It was in early '81, fresh off the UK success that we were in bigger venues finally and had the clout to demand the shows be all-ages. Critics ridiculed it as a gimmick. But those kids started hardcore bands and the critics were out of a job." The trip also proved a financial disaster. "We went to New York and lost our shirt on the flights," notes Ray. "When I got back, Bob Last [founder of Edinburgh's Fast Product] called me and said he wanted to put 'California' out."

"Jim Fouratt of a club called Hurrah's had hosted Bob in New York and played him a whole bunch of records," Biafra recalls. "The ones that Bob Last liked the most were 'California Über Alles', Middle Class's debut EP and another San Francisco duo called Noh Mercy. Those were the three he dug. And 'California Über Alles' already existed as a kick-ass single so he had something to release without having to record or pay for it. I was pretty blown away, because I grasped how important Fast Product was at that time. People were waiting with bated breath for the next Fast single after he'd sprung the Gang of Four, the Mekons, Human League, Scars and others. Bob Last deserves a thank you. Without him, Dead Kennedys would have been gone within a year and a half."

"I felt like I was swept into it because it all happened so quickly," says Klaus. "All of us probably had the feeling of that in some way. We had some slow times; our first East Coast tour was a dreadful mess. When we came back from it, things picked up again." Indeed, no-one in the band has particularly fond memories of this period. "We'd done an East Coast tour and gone to New York as total unknowns," remembers Biafra. "It might have been too soon. I went through culture shock. Some of the other guys . . . you start to learn a little bit more about everybody that way, and I wasn't liking what I was seeing. The guys who'd played in bar bands were acting like that again, and I was like, well, maybe we're done, but I'll wait and see if the single goes anywhere. Then it did! I knew it was a really good record, the songs were good, and the sound itself was more powerful than a lot of other home-made punk singles coming out at that time."

Last, whose Fast Product did indeed produce a near peerless run of singles before he safeguarded the label's mystique by closing the label early, remembers it slightly differently. "Jim Fouratt was a good friend at the time. I went over to New York and stayed with him, but actually Dead Kennedys was completely coincidental to that. Noh Mercy and Middle Class were both things that [critic] Jon Savage drew to my attention, which I loved. The Dead Kennedys I think I heard – I'm not sure that John Peel didn't call me up. At that time we were very close with Peel. I probably phoned him up during his show – 'Who the fuck are these people – what is their number?' That's my recollection." Biafra admits he can't recall whether Last called him and mentioned Fouratt first or vice versa.

In one of the band's first mainstream press notices, *Sounds* proclaimed the single "Wagnerian punk with production as dirty as a bear's bum". 'California' was to be the label's final release, despite it being its most successful. "I can remember thinking it was a really funny, cool song," recalls Jon Langford of fellow Fast artists the Mekons, "but we were in the throes of moving off Fast to a major – Bob was very keen on that. I got the impression he was pretty over running a label." Last confirms that to be the case. "We just picked 'California' up because it was the perfect thing to end that series of singles on – you couldn't have had a better high to go out on. My partner Hillary and I did have some discussion about doing an album, but it wasn't that I wasn't interested in their album, it was that I wasn't interested enough in *albums* at that time. It wasn't what the label was about; it was about these special moments." According to Biafra, "Bob Last did offer to follow the single with a 12-inch EP, but we didn't want to do that. We had enough good songs for an album and America needed another strong underground punk album. Only the Germs had done it. We even looked into getting Kenny Laguna to produce us because the Germs' LP sounded so good, but it didn't happen."

"It all came together, with Biafra and Klaus and 6025 and Ted through serendipity," says Ray. "Everybody was at the right place at the right time. First with 'California Über Alles' as a single, then Biafra ran for mayor, which was a great gimmick. We kind of became the number one punk band in San Francisco, even though we were really the third generation one." Biafra remains adamant that serendipity, to use Ray's vernacular, and happenstance were key to the DKs becoming Californian punk's hottest export. "It was something that we had to handle very carefully in the hometown. Here we'd had this random stroke of luck that had eluded the Avengers, Dils, X, Weirdos on down. I've always tried to look at that and keep reminding myself that it wasn't necessarily because we were the best band at the time, it was just pure, dumb luck."

Dead Kennedys continued to play wherever it could, insisting on under-ages shows and DIY booking themselves. As Michael Azerrad would later point out in *Our Band Could Be Your Life*, it was Canada's DOA and the DKs who "became the Lewis and Clarks of the punk touring circuit, blazing a trail across America that bands still follow today". Or as Black Flag's Greg Ginn put it in the same book, "With those bands we did a lot of networking, sharing information. We'd find a new place to play, then we'd let them know because they were interested in going wherever they could and playing. Then we would help each other in our own towns." Hence Black Flag would support Dead Kennedys at the Mabuhay Gardens on 10 October 1979, a gig that Joe Nolte of The Last would record in his journal. "The only thing I knew about the Dead Kennedys was that their singer, Jello Biafra, was running for mayor. The other three members of the band came onstage looking about as menacing as The Crickets. Then Jello bounced out and pandemonium ensued. Those fuckers were *great* – one of the best hardcore bands I've seen in a while. Jello would antagonize and fall into the crowd à la Darby [Crash, of the Germs], except that, unlike Darby, he *never* lost control, *never* stopped singing . . . controlled chaos."[7]

It's important to remember that the DKs' stature would have much to do with their overseas reception. In an age when many American critics had Anglophile

MAN WITH THE DOGS

DEAD KENNEDYS

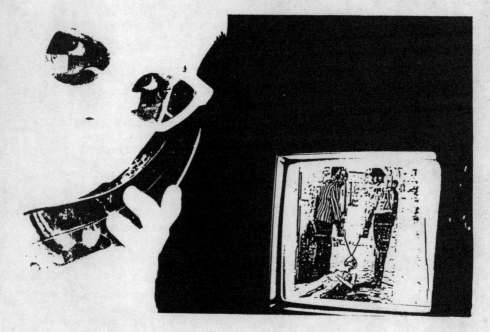

THE DEAD KENNEDYS (California Uber Alles/The Man with the Dogs)
Alternative Tentacles Records

"Alles" is a very apparent parody. This months great gimmick record, it should replace "Rock Lobster" in college dorm rooms as a hip single. With a name like Dead Kennedys I expected a lot more than a Jerry Brown as Hitler parody. But I did get more. The music for example — it's not your standard punk slam. True the guitar distort is on full throttle but there's a wierd echoplex warp device too, the drummers rhythms are closer to jazz than to 4/4 slam slam and lead crooner Jello Biafra has a bizzare Bryan Ferry type warble to his high pitched voice. Sweet and nasty. "Alles" has always been a high point of the Kennedys great live performance and though I find the mix too guitar heavy, the impact has not been lost in the vinyl transfer process. You know what? I like "Man with the Dogs" even better. More driving, more sarcastic fun and a great line, "What's inside is a pubic hair, a cobweb there, but you just don't care". The Dead Kennedys are much more than this year's political gimmick joke band. They are more than the Eighties answer to Country Joe and the Fish. In fact they might be one of the most important bands to come out of this scene. This single gives you all the clues as to why...

Z.

Previous pages: 'California Über Alles' / 'Man With The Dogs' – US release 1979 first + second pressing (Alternative Tentacles / Optional Music)

Above: Single review + Gig listing, *Slash* Magazine Vol. 2 No. 9, October 1979

Right: 'California Über Alles' / 'Man With The Dogs' – UK release 1979 (Fast Product)

WARning

It is remarkable that we are willing to sacrifice for a war but we won't sacrifice to avoid a war.

It is remarkable that we are willing to kill & die in order to keep our cars on the road. But what good is a car if you're dead? What good is a car if you can't afford to fill it with that precious gasoline?

It is remarkable that we are willing to spend billions of dollars on a massive war effort to "protect" oil fields that are no more ours than they are the Russians'.

It is remarkable that we will spend billions on war when we could spend that money on developing our own energy resources and on becoming independant and self sufficient.

Multinational corporations are virtually states unto themselves. They are not bound by the borders and laws of any one nation. They are neither constrained by our laws nor concerned with the welfare of the American people. Therefore it is remarkable that we let the "Vital Interests" of corporations, which are not even American, dictate foreign policy that will eventually erode our civil rights and conscript men and women into the armed forces to fight a war for corporate profit rather than such traditional American ideals as freedom & liberty.

It is remarkable that any thinking individual could join or let himself be drafted into an army whose administration has consistently ignored the plight of most Viet Nam veterans regarding unemployment and VA benefits from army inflicted disorders resulting in exposure to Agent Orange and atomic bomb testing.

It is especially remarkable that America seems willing to hand over the lives of their children in order to keep the transnationals out of the red and their microwaves in the black. We are a very obliging people. Up till now our autos have been running on corporate oil. Soon they will be running on the blood of our own children.

Right: Poster designed by Jamie Reid to promote 'California Über Alles'. Though the imagery mixes *Triumph Of The Will* with a reminder of Altamont thuggery, Reid actually used a photograph from the Reading Festival. The design of this poster also coincided with Reid's work for the Sex Pistols film *The Great Rock 'n' Roll Swindle* – as evidenced in the cannabis swastikas and 'Never Trust A Hippie' footnote.

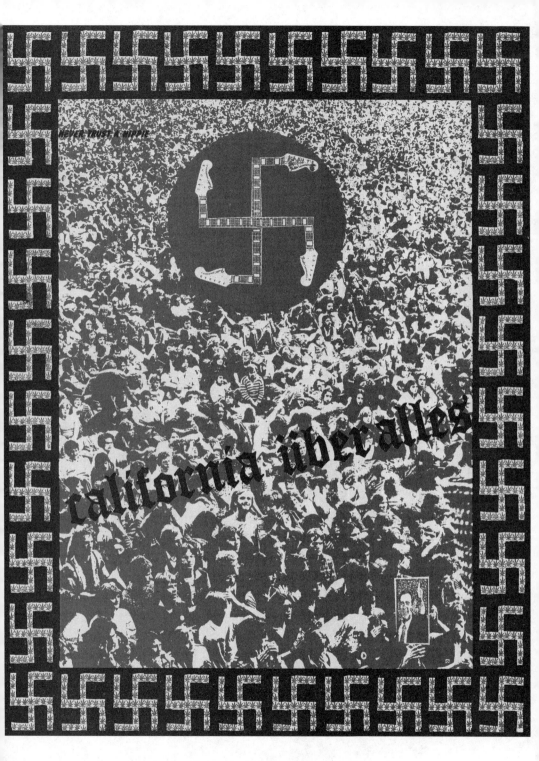

NEVER TRUST A HIPPIE

california über alles

tendencies, it meant that the DKs had an international gravitas that peers such as DOA, Black Flag and Minor Threat could not initially match. The buzz around the band in the UK that followed the release of 'California Über Alles' was therefore welcome. However, there was some degree of consternation at the emergence of a highly-politicised punk band from 'sunny' California at a time when opinion formers had concluded that punk's slide was terminal – though that was never Biafra's view. "There was a whole other generation rumbling right beneath the surface that exploded the very next year. Everybody from the Crass label bands to Discharge to the Riot City bands and the others, they were right below the surface. But the British music press wasn't interested and wasn't paying attention to it." There was good reason for that. Some of the releases on Crass were extraordinary and Discharge did indeed up the ante; much of the rest was mush.

Coincidentally, Dead Kennedys would secure a high profile show supporting punk warhorses The Clash at Kezar Pavilion on 13 October 1979. "That was a very big show for us," remembers Ray, "and we were in the hallway looking at the private dressing room. It was one of the few shows that Biafra lost his pants. Which gave us no end of notoriety. But very scary for him, I would imagine. It wasn't planned or part of the act." Promoter Bill Graham was so outraged by Jello's nudity he vowed that the Dead Kennedys would never appear on one of his stages again, and was as good as his word. "I jumped into the crowd and came back with only my belt, my boots, and my Argyle socks intact," Biafra recalls. "So I did the rest of the show nude. From what I was told afterwards, Bill Graham had to be physically restrained from going on stage and beating the crap out of me. But Bill Graham didn't ban us. We just refused to work for him. It was the last time we ever played for him. Boy, am I glad of that. I know he has a good reputation in some circles, but certainly not underground punk circles at the time. He was very heavy-handed and had monopolistic practices whereby any show that wasn't Bill Graham wasn't supposed to exist in the San Francisco Bay Area." A rumour went round that he destroyed an entire print run of the first Nuns record when he heard 'Decadent Jew', without realising that it was written by Jewish band member Jeff Olener and was intended to debunk stereotypes (Biafra disputes the potential of this happening). "But when there was money to be made," Biafra concludes, "of course he came round, and booked Hüsker Dü. Even the Screamers got booked once by Bill Graham."

As for seeing The Clash up front, Biafra was unmoved. "I'd seen them before," Biafra recalls. "I can't remember if I really watched much of them the night we played

Above left: DKs Live – Victory 1978. (Photograph by Ruby Ray)
Below left: DKs Live – Defeat 1978. Biafra was regularly pantsed after that. (Photograph by Ruby Ray)

with them. We'd sort of got a bad taste in our mouths because they took a four-hour sound-check. Showing they were men of the people by giving little kids the guitars to play 'Louie Louie' while The Cramps and Dead Kennedys and Rockabilly Rebels waited for a sound-check that was never allowed. Then they went back to the hotel, and only came back right before they went on stage. It was not really a pivotal moment in the history of Dead Kennedys."

Above right: Climbing the Amps, 1978. Jello Biafra and Joe Rees of Target in front. (Photograph by Ruby Ray)
Below right: DKs Live – Crazy Dance, 1978. Biafra had some crazy moves that the audience would imitate. (Photograph by Ruby Ray)

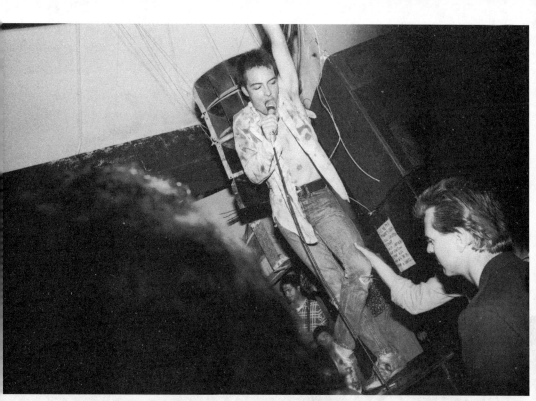

BLACK FLAG

'20 minutes' respite from the sanctuary of sleep'

at Mabuhay Gardens Wed. Oct. 10 with
the Dead Kennedys

"There's a vice cop in every daisy chain"

Black Flag E.P. Available From: SST Records; P.O. Box 1, Lawndale Calif. 90260

Raymond Pettibone Black Flag Flyer #16 noted libellist

62

So You're Skeptical?

BIAFRA® for MAYOR
Campaign Fund Raiser

SYMPTOMS
ANTI-BODIES
EYE PROTECTION
VS. JARS
CONTRACTIONS
PINK SECTION
DEAD KENNEDYS

SEPT. 3 **LABOR DAY** **MABUHAY**

Chapter 4

Are You Believin' the Morning Papers?

Driving to pick up his son, Bennie alternated between The Sleepers and
the Dead Kennedys, San Francisco bands he'd grown up with.
(from Jennifer Egan's *A Visit From The Goon Squad,* featuring a
chapter on the Fab Mab, which won the 2011 Pulitzer Prize)

Biafra was by now, clothed or otherwise, already the consummate front-man. "I come from a theatre background. I like mood. I like vibe. I like characters. I didn't realise for years how much the method acting I went through influenced both the music and lyrics I write, and how I match them up. When it comes to production and mixing I'm more like a film director, more interested in vibe or mood than each instrument being perfect. The lyrics are very visual, often, a 'you are there' scenario, instead of ranting and raving about a particular subject I have opinions on." Back home in Boulder, in a delectable piece of casting, he'd previously appeared as the lead Nazi in a high school production of *The Sound Of Music,* as well as playing the Boris Karloff role in *Arsenic And Old Lace.* "Some of my best moments on stage are when the characters do come to life from inside me, and I can see parts of where the character is at in my mind's eyes."

It also gave Dead Kennedys an immediate visual signature. "I realised early on that I should bring out parts of myself that I didn't see in the main 'visionaries' of other bands," he continues. "There were voids I could fill. I was more theatrical on stage than any other singer I knew of in San Francisco. I saw a distinct lack of that and tried to fill that hole, but at the same time get some Stooges and Germs energy into the mix as well. I still do that, it's the same thing I do today." Similarly he was keen to mark out lyrical turf away from his peers. "I try to write songs about things other people haven't already written about. Granted, the Circle Jerks and [the Washington, DC] Youth Brigade came out with songs about the Moral Majority at the same time I wrote mine, but in the long run I knew mine was going to be the most cruel . . ."

The theatrics went hand in hand with a lifelong devotion to troublemaking. Never as po-faced as some critics maintain, Biafra always enjoyed a mischievous wheeze – for more on which you are directed to his interview in RE/Search Publications' *Pranks!* compendium. However, it was his mayoral challenge in the fall of 1979 that won him most notoriety. A benefit for his campaign was held on Labor Day in early September. The Symptoms, Anti-Bodies, Eye Protection, Contractions and Pink Section were among the support bands, which together with a spaghetti banquet raised a budget of $1,500. The Mabuhay was synonymous with cheap spag-bol, as nutritious a meal as many local punks could afford, as well as late-night music, so it all seemed appropriate. Most of the budget went on buying a place on the ballot. "If a person doesn't get enough petition signatures to run for local office in San Francisco," says Biafra, "they can make up the difference by paying something like $10 a head." The manifesto was written on a napkin while watching a Pere Ubu concert – after Ted had ribbed him about having such a big mouth he should stand for electoral office.

His policies had several strands, including hiring laid-off city workers as panhandlers at 50% commission to replace funds lost through the deeply unpopular Proposition 13 tax dodge. This particularly irksome slice of legislature appeased property owners while ballooning the state's budget deficit by fixing the maximum tax take to 1% of any property's cash value – assessed at 1975 values. "It is actually popular to the point of being sacred now," Biafra updates us. "Thus the state is bankrupt." Police would have to stand at elections, and squatting would be legalised in disused buildings. A Board of Bribery would be established to set 'influence' rates. Most enterprising of all Biafra's manifesto commitments, downtown businessmen would have to dress as clowns between the hours of nine to five. Despite this, Biafra's manifesto was supported by the most unlikely of sources; but then Sheriff Mike Hennessey was a huge fan of punk rock and a regular at the Fab Mab. Only in San Francisco . . .

'There's always room for Jello' was one of the campaign catch-phrases (parodying an actual 1964 advertising strap-line used by Jell-O's manufacturers, Kraft), as well as 'Apocalypse Now, Vote for Biafra' and the simple but emphatic 'What if he wins?' Other coups included vacuuming leaves from the front lawn of opponent Dianne Feinstein's lawn (debunking her publicity stunt of sweeping 'Frisco streets). "I did it because ever since I was about six or seven," Biafra related, "I discovered I had a peculiar talent for annoying people and I got more and more interested in perfecting ways to do it over the years."

The headliners for a second benefit show were British band The Members, who were on their first tour of America. "We were playing a gig through the FBI booking agency run by Ian Copeland at the Waldorf Ballroom," remembers vocalist Nicky Tesco, "We turned up to play and Jello was down the front going bananas! We'd heard of Dead Kennedys and he came backstage, and boy, can he talk! I really liked Jello. The times I spent in San Francisco hanging out with him were brilliant. Jello wanted to do a fundraiser, so he asked us if we were up for it. That was at a place in Geary Street, a de-sanctified synagogue (The Temple) where a lot of punk events took place. We said yeah, let's do it. It was probably the best gig we did on that tour – because it wasn't a bar or club, younger people were able to get in and it raised quite a lot of money. That night Jello and I went out drinking, and that was a blast. He took me to this place where there was a long narrow bar, and I wasn't really paying attention – and I'm not at all homophobic – but I must have clocked that I was in a gay bar. I looked behind the bar and saw a middle-aged woman in a Dior dress and ... she had a beard. Jello was always very focused. It was quite difficult times – America wasn't London. America has a lot of crazies walking round, but Jello would really speak his mind. All the crazies in America head west, and when they reach California they can't go any further. And if you read the things he said, Jello was very prescient and very articulate. A lot of his lyrics were highly intelligent; I remember him being funny and sharp. Still to this day me and my kids play 'Cambodia' and 'California Über Alles.'"

The upshot was that Jello came fourth of ten candidates in the November poll with 3.79% of the vote and more than 6,500 votes. Feinstein's campaign manager was heard to bemoan the fact that if "someone like *that*" could achieve such a turnout, "this city is in real trouble". Feinstein held office for ten years before becoming a Democratic senator. In a strange twist of DKs' related trivia, she officiated at Jerry Brown's 2005 wedding, and was all set to run against him until pulling out of the race for governor in February 2010.

More importantly, Biafra's candidature proved a focal point for the San Francisco underground and punk community (*Damage* fanzine editor Lap would crow: "We have our own paper, our own television station [Target] and our own candidate for mayor"). Whether directly related or not, a welter of new bands formed and found themselves with new venues to play beyond the Fab Mab: X's, The Hotel Utah, Rock City, The Back Dor, etc. There was a symbiotic resurgence in local performance and visual media hosted at 'art clubs' such as the A-Hole and Club Generic. All of these developments may well have occurred without the mayoral campaign or Dead Kennedys; but it didn't hurt. However, despite the notoriety of the campaign, and the immediate success of 'California Über Alles', Biafra maintains that at this time, Dead Kennedys were only just moving ahead of The Dils and Mutants in local popularity.

"My memory of Jello Biafra as a performer is that he interacted with the audience more than a lot of punk singers," notes author Jennifer Egan, who watched the band at several Fab Mab shows and elsewhere. "He'd leap into the audience and get passed around for quite a while before returning to stage. I seem to recall his pants being torn off on at least one of these occasions – an exciting thing for a high school girl to witness! I was at that [supporting The Clash at Kezar] show. My sense is that Jello was less troubled than a lot of the punk singers – he had energy and vitality, a kind of playfulness that was very different from, say, Ricky Sleeper. Jello didn't seem genuinely angry or depressed. I have no idea what his drug use was like, but I'm guessing he wasn't a junkie. The fact that he ran for mayor of San Francisco also suggested a broader vision than a lot of punk singers seemed to have."

The success of 'California Über Alles' also earned the group an appearance at San Francisco's BAMMIE Awards on 25 March 1980. "*Bay Area Musician*, or *BAM* for short, was kind of the *Rolling Stone* for San Francisco," Ray recalls. "It would have these award shows every year. You get to give an award to people and that strokes their ego. That's what the BAMMIES were about. As a journalist, one of your biggest fears is being uncool. And the BAMMIES figured they were being uncool, because The Clash were coming. All this stuff was coming out in England, all this new music in the Top Ten. And there's nothing like that in the States. So they asked us to play, in order to give themselves some street cred, I guess. And of course, we were meant to play our big hit, 'California Über Alles'. But we changed it a bit, and it became 'Pull My Strings.'"

Dead Kennedys took the stage at the Warfield Theatre in 'new wave' attire, comprising white shirts emblazoned with a large 'S'. During the intro to their 'hit single', Biafra took the microphone. "Hold it. We've got to prove we're adults now. We're not a punk band, we're a new wave band!" The differentiation in genre affiliation – not explicit in Ray's original band advert – is important to note. The American incarnation of 'new wave' was regarded as a dilution, a way for the biz to continue selling records with a decorative coating of fake 'edge'. "The BAMMIES acknowledged new wave because of the runaway success of The Knack," Biafra elaborates. The latter's insipid new wave was widely derided within the punk community as a paradigm of this hybrid, right through to a jokey 'Nuke the Knack' campaign. Thin black ties were then draped over the band's shirts to form a dollar sign, the parody completed by the opening chords to 'My Sharona', rechristened 'My Payola'. Biafra goaded the bemused audience to sing along. Ray played a fine hand too, regurgitating a thoroughly loathsome guitar solo, Hendrix-style, teeth and all, while his compatriots stood around yawning. "'Pull My Strings' is also the only song where Ted wrote the music," Biafra adds. "I think I did give him the lyrics ahead of time. We needed a new wave song so I turned to the guy in the band who most wanted us to be more pop! And he really came through."

Among the audience members to witness these surreal events (later voted the 26th greatest 'rock moment' of all time in the *NME*) were Carlos Santana, Jerry Garcia, Ronnie Montrose, Francis Ford Coppola, Eddie Money, Boz Scaggs and Journey. "That was a different world we hated so much we didn't want anything to do with it," notes Biafra, who maintains that the stunt was his idea and the rest of the band were resistant to it, but "had fun with it" in the end. Scaggs was particularly outraged, and Coppola allegedly shoved Ted into a wall as he passed him backstage; though both Money and Journey drummer Steve Smith saw the funny side and congratulated Biafra on the evening's antics afterwards.

The live recording of 'Pull My Strings' was another early period Dead Kennedys recording to see release on the posthumous compilation *Give Me Convenience Or Give Me Death*. It had provisionally been intended to combine it as part of a live four-song 12-inch with the *Urgh! A Music War* movie versions of 'Chemical Warfare', 'Government Flu' and 'Bleed For Me', which were filmed in August 1980 but ended up missing the soundtrack cut (though the latter track was appended to the 2009 DVD release on Warners). The film, produced by Miles Copeland, has stunning footage, if you can forgive the poorly synchronised crowd shots. And it's interesting to note the lyrics to 'Bleed For Me' attacking Rosalynn Carter, the then First Lady. Ronald Reagan – aka 'Cowboy Ronnie' – would be the subject of the released version, but he was then only a month on from securing the Republican nomination – evidence, once again, that Biafra liked to keep his words contemporaneous.

Above: Portion of a collage by Winston Smith from *Fuck Facts* #1, a newspaper of collage art included with the Dead Kennedys album *Bedtime For Democracy*

Above right: East Bay Ray 1978. (Photograph by Ruby Ray)

Below right: DKs Live On the Floor 1978. (Photograph by Ruby Ray)

Overleaf above left: Dead Kennedys at the BAMMIES. (Illustration by Vasilia Dimitrova)

72

Overleaf: Pages from Dead Kennedys 'Hard Rock' comic, originally published by Revolutionary Comics. Words by Deena Dasein, artwork by Joe Paradise, stuff by Jay Allen Sanford.

JELLO WAS A PRODUCT OF THE '60'S — WHEN THE BROTHERS KENNEDY WERE KILLED AND YOUTH WAS POLITICAL.

I'M LOOKING FORWARD TO TONIGHT'S PERE UBU SHOW.

I'M GONNA RUN FOR *MAYOR*?

GO FOR IT!

THE BACK COVER OF THE OCTOBER 1979 ISSUE OF *DAMAGE* FANZINE DELIVERS THE NEWS.

GET THIS! BIAFRA'S RUNNING FOR MAYOR OF SAN FRANCISCO!

WHAT A WAY TO CELEBRATE THE WESTERN FRONT FESTIVAL!

JELLO CAMPAIGNS AROUND SAN FRANCISCO!

IF HE DOESN'T WIN... I'LL KILL MYSELF

WHAT IF HE WINS?

DIRK DIRKSEN HOSTS A BENEFIT AT THE MABUHAY TO RAISE FUNDS FOR THE CAMPAIGN.

I WILL HIRE LAID-OFF CITY WORKERS TO PANHANDLE AT 50% COMMISSION TO REPLACE FUNDS LOST THROUGH PROPOSITION 13!

POLICE WILL HAVE TO BE ELECTED!

AND I'LL CLEAN UP MARKET STREET BY REQUIRING BUSINESSMEN TO WEAR CLOWN SUITS BETWEEN NINE AND FIVE!

WE WILL ERECT *DAN WHITE* STATUES AROUND TOWN *AND* HAVE CONCESSION STANDS SELLING EGGS AND TOMATOES TO *THROW* AT THOSE STATUES!

WE'LL BAN AUTOMOBILES DOWNTOWN, AND IMPOSE RENT CONTROL TO THWART THOSE GREEDY LANDLORDS!

AND WE'LL HAVE A BOARD OF BRIBERY TO SET "INFLUENCE" RATES.

ALTHOUGH HE WAS UNDERAGE, RAN UNDER A FALSE NAME, AND SPENT AN UNGRAND TOTAL OF $1500 ON THE CAMPAIGN, JELLO BIAFRA FINISHED 4TH IN A FIELD OF 10, GETTING 6,591 VOTES.

BIAFRA

SAYS A LOT ABOUT THE *OTHER* 9 CANDIDATES, HUH?

⑦

THE ELECTION IS OVER BUT THE POLITICS GO ON. A DEAD KENNEDYS GIG IN VANCOUVER, NOVEMBER 22, 1979:

HEY, ISN'T TODAY...?

YEP, THE ANNIVERSARY OF JFK'S ASSASSINATION.

THIS IS FOR CALIFORNIA'S GOVERNOR JERRY BROWN.

IT'S CALLED "CALIFORNIA ÜBER ALLES".

HEY—WHERE'S OL' 6025? MUST'VE QUIT THE BAND!

PUNKY

MORE SONG SUBJECTS INCLUDE PATTY HEARST'S KIDNAPPING, AMONG OTHER UNCONVENTIONAL INSPIRATIONS.

MR. EAST BAY RAY, WOULDN'T YOU SAY THAT A DEAD KENNEDYS SHOW IS IN BAD TASTE?

OF COURSE IT'S IN BAD TASTE!

BUT THE ASSASSINATIONS WEREN'T TOO "TASTEFUL" EITHER!!

THIS IS GREAT! THE SUCCESS OF "CALIFORNIA ÜBER ALLES" GOT US INVITED TO PERFORM AT THE BAMMIES!

WHAT'S THE BAMMIES?

THE FRISCO GRAMMIES! IT'S THE BAY AREA MAGAZINE'S AWARD CEREMONY.

YEAH, A BACK-SLAPPING CIRCUS BANQUET!

THE PLACE'LL BE FULL OF INDUSTRY BIG-WIGS AND HORRID ACTS LIKE JOURNEY!

LET'S DO SOMETHING REALLY INTERESTING!

ONSTAGE AT THE BAMMIES...

THEY THINK WE'RE GONNA DO "CALIFORNIA ÜBER ALLES" LIKE WE DID AT DRESS REHEARSAL!

WAIT'LL THEY HEAR OUR ATTACK ON THE MUSIC INDUSTRY· COMPOSED ESPECIALLY FOR THIS OCCASION*!

*"PULL MY STRINGS"

AFTERWARDS:

I DON'T THINK WE'LL BE INVITED BACK!

WHO CARES! WE DON'T NEED NO GOOD-WILL FROM A BUNCH OF BAY AREA MAGAZINES!

WANNA BET?

⑧

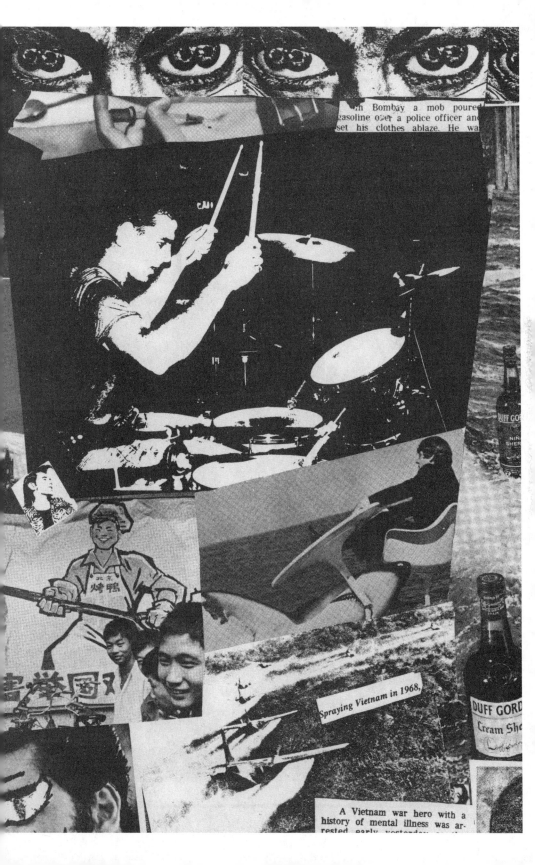

Spraying Vietnam in 1968,

A Vietnam war hero with a history of mental illness was arrested early yesterday

Chapter 5

Anyone Can Be King for a Day

Seek not the favour of the multitude; it is seldom got by honest and lawful means.
But seek the testimony of few; and number not voices, but weigh them.
(Immanuel Kant)

Matters were moving quickly in the UK. "Bill Gilliam called and said, 'Do you guys want to tour England?'" Ray recalls. "We said, sure. Then he called back and said, 'It's hard to tour on a single. Have you got enough stuff for an LP?' Sure. Then he put Iain [McNay, Cherry Red co-founder] in touch with me, and we worked it out from there." Gilliam had originally discovered the band via three tracks, 'Police Truck', 'Short Songs' and 'Straight A's' on the *Live At The Deaf Club* compilation, recorded in October 1979.[8] He takes up the story. "I used to be a booking agent for people like Sham 69. And while I was doing Sham 69 I was sniffing round this band from the States with this silly name. I just thought it would be fun to get them over here. Eventually I got them the deal with Cherry Red. Before that I got thrown out of just about every record company without them even hearing the tapes." Gilliam would eventually head up the UK division of the band's Alternative Tentacles label.

That wasn't the only interest in the UK, nor the only Sham 69 connection. "Tony Gordon [their manager, and later behind the success of Culture Club *et al*] was also pursuing us after he saw us open for Sham 69 at the Whiskey in LA," Biafra recalls. "He was blown away. He was proposing we come to the UK and tour with Sham and record the album live at the Marquee, to be released on Safari! [a small independent label set up by Deep Purple's former management team whose key act would be Toyah]. Can you imagine what a disaster *that* would have been? At the height of Sham's hooligan problem? We didn't know any better. Luckily we chose Cherry Red because they were the only ones offering a full *studio* album."

Iain McNay first met Gilliam through Chris Gilbert, manager of the Hollywood Brats, and Gilliam's partner in a booking and management agency in Westbourne Grove. Gilbert called McNay to say Gilliam was working with a band called Dead

Left: Biafra for Mayor 1978. Campaign poster. (Photograph by Ruby Ray)
Pages 76-77: Portions of the collage poster given away with *Fresh Fruit For Rotting Vegetables*, designed by Jello Biafra.

Kennedys. "I was obviously aware of the band," McNay recalls, "because they had 'California Über Alles' out through Fast Product, and I'd heard that and really liked it." Gilliam explained that the band had asked for $10,000 to do an album (Biafra believes it was $8,000). "I said 'I'm definitely interested' and went off to think about it. I got to hear a demo of the original version of 'Holiday In Cambodia', which I wish I'd kept. I heard that and thought – that's great. I just knew the album would do so well. I didn't have the $10,000 at that stage, because Cherry Red was in a formative stage. So I was wondering how I was going to get this $10,000, but I didn't tell Bill that. My only other reservation was, I liked the name Dead Kennedys, because it was controversial, but I wondered whether that was going to block me too much for radio play or anything else."

He got over that. "I mused and decided I was fine with the name and I'd get beyond that OK," McNay continues. "I had a close relationship in those days with Caroline Records, a Virgin-owned export company. I was having lunch one day with the buyer, Richard Bishop, and chatting about my dilemma, that I had an opportunity with Dead Kennedys, but I didn't have the money to pay them what they wanted. Richard said, 'Maybe there's a deal where we give you the money, and you give us a good price on export, and a three-month exclusive, which means during that time you wouldn't sell to any other exporter.' I thought, that's not a bad idea. So we ended up doing the deal and Caroline gave me the $10,000." McNay, as anyone with experience of working with him will attest, is not one to bet the farm on a single artist, and not for the first or last time he'd successfully spread the risk of his involvement with a project. The investment would become the defining moment in the label's early history prior to its *Pillows & Prayers* era, when Mike Alway took over its A&R, and set the foundations for what remains one of the most successful longstanding UK independent labels.

"When I was in America," remembers McNay, "I saw them play a college date about an hour and a half hour's drive from San Francisco. I remember the whole thing being very raw and shambolic. The sound was very, very raw. The whole evening was shambolic. But that was punk and that was Dead Kennedys. The tour in the UK all went fine. It's not as if they had the problems that the Sex Pistols had or anything. The dates happened, there was a good turnout, and a minimum of trouble from what I remember."

In the meantime, the band busied themselves with a second single, and managed to outdo themselves. 'Holiday In Cambodia' crystallises so much of what Dead Kennedys were about. At its heart lay Olympic-standard sarcasm at the complacency of Middle America and its 'me' generation, tracing a direct line through to the in-equity of its foreign policy. But the constructs are defiantly non-linear. Elementary school perennial Dr Seuss story *The Sneetches* is invoked in reference to star-bellied sneetches and invidious hierarchies and the merry-go-round of envy and conformity. "And I figured sneetch also rhymed with leech," Biafra concedes, generously.

The music conveys a congruent sense of jeopardy and revulsion. Klaus's chilling bass hum sets the stage for Ray's guitar, dropping in and out of the rhythm before ripping away on a series of tack-sharp leads. That sense of heightened menace is attributed by Ray to the use of a 'flatted fifth'– achieved by playing a dissonant fifth note half an octave removed in a chord sequence. It is a technique common to both bebop jazz and hard rock but also known as the 'devil's interval' (*diabolus in musica*). Medieval musicians were hanged for using it: priests believed it destroyed the fabric or consonance of the perfect octave. The song's conclusion is fevered, the whole piece flawlessly arranged. "I didn't realise it at the time," says Klaus, "but that bass section; it was two different things, basically. There was the Velvet Underground thing of having the droned A-string, like in 'Venus In Furs'. It's got this constant drone going on in it. It was that feel, and also Led Zeppelin. I'd just realised what I'd done subconsciously was speed up that Zeppelin riff and throw it against a drone. Nothing in music is completely original, unless you go into John Cage land. I was just taking the roots and mutating them."

"That was one of the few times the band put together a song as a unit," confirms Biafra, "and it wasn't just one member bringing in the whole song, and that's probably why it's so good. I brought in an original 'Holiday In Cambodia' that was more of a Ramones-style chainsaw punk song. Ray and Klaus said they didn't like it and didn't want to play it, and I was very hurt and very upset – this had never happened before. Then Klaus started playing that bass line the same day while I'd stepped out of the garage. And I ran back and said, wait a minute – slow down 'Holiday In Cambodia', take away my verse-riff, put that one in, and use the original pre-chorus, chorus and the bridge, and this could be a really cool song. And sure enough it was . . . Ray couldn't come up with a part. I kept saying, 'Ray, think Syd Barrett!' Then finally Ray found that guitar part that he has over Klaus's bass at the beginning of the verses, and 'Holiday In Cambodia', as we know it, was born."

The inspiration for the lyrics to 'Holiday In Cambodia' may surprise somewhat. "I wrote it in Boulder before I moved to San Francisco," states Biafra. "It was basically a reaction against me delivering pizzas to really spoiled, drunk college students at the University of Colorado for a year and a half. I thought that would be a good thing to do to them. It's the same clowns who inspired 'Terminal Preppie' [on *Plastic Surgery Disasters*] as well, if you want to call it inspiration. They're the people I wrote both songs about."

Geza X, aka Geza Gedeon, either as producer or engineer, shaped the early Californian punk sound through releases by the Germs, Avengers, Black Flag and X, as well as playing with The Bags and Deadbeats. "I would have been in my late twenties, I guess," he recalls. "In some cases five to ten years older than everyone else. I already had some street chops. I was a radical in the '60s, doing draft counselling when I was fourteen and an underground newspaper at my high school. I already had a lot of ideas on how to mobilise people. When punk rock came up I threw my heart into that. I was always interested in recording, but I hadn't done very much. I was room-mates with Joe Nanini and Stan Ridgeway of Wall of Voodoo before punk. We were playing at various clubs and cafes and it was just ridiculous – you could not turn up an amplifier or everyone would freak out. So we were hungry for loud music. Joe came in one day with a Ramones record; we just listened to it all the way through and flipped out. Then the same thing happened pretty soon after that with the Sex Pistols record. Anyway, I listened to the Ramones and I saw it right away. Then Joe and I were immediately trying to get into a punk rock band. We went and saw some bands – the Weirdos, the Screamers – and were just genuinely thrilled. The Germs were also around already. I spoke to Brendan [Mullen, founder of famed LA punk venue The Masque] and asked if I could rent a small space there. I became the sound man and Brendan's right-hand person. I did the Germs, my bands The Deadbeats and The Bags [on Dangerhouse Records] and those went far and wide in California. A lot of bands wanted to talk to me after that. I was also a lot of people's house engineer, going up and down the coast – going to San Francisco and mixing bands at Mabuhay Gardens and other places. And that's also how people got to know me. When they saw the records word just got around. The whole punk contingent was relatively small. They were all into the same records – the 45s that came from England or New York or LA."

His link to Dead Kennedys came "almost out of nowhere" but was tangentially connected to Biafra's then favourites, the Screamers. "I was the Screamers' kind of roadie and soundman, and I went everywhere the Screamers went. We went frequently to San Francisco. Target Video began to video these bands." Target, founded by Joe Rees, quickly established itself at the heart of the Californian underground, its black building home to three floors whose editing, recording and video studios and punk rock jukebox made it a natural 'clubhouse' for the emergent San Francisco punk scene.

"They loved the Screamers," Geza explains, "because that was the number one art band. We'd go with the Screamers to do a live video shoot and I'd mix the sound, and those things turned out pretty nice, most of them. We were doing one of these video shoots and got invited to lunch by these kids who I thought had just graduated school [Biafra believes this to be he and Carlos]. They told us this crazy pipe dream that they had of a band they were going to start called Dead Kennedys. I thought, 'Wow, that's a pretty good name!' They were going to just *rage* at you – they were all enthusiasm. I made a mental note of the name and I got a chance to go back maybe a month or two later. And who was headlining the Mabuhay but Dead Kennedys? So I had to see them. I was standing right in front of the PA monitors – I'll never forget this – and Dead Kennedys come on and play 'Holiday In Cambodia'. I'm getting chills right now, I don't know how many years later, talking about it. My hair just stood on end. I was hearing this song come off the stage, and watching Biafra, this amazing front-person. I thought, my God, this song's a hit. This is unbelievable. These guys are great! I was laughing, I couldn't believe that these kids who came up with this wild idea, this crazy fantasy, could have been one of the best bands I had seen on the West Coast *ever*. They were so good already. They were phenomenal. I would have been a nut not to cut that song! I got a phone call a few weeks later, unsolicited. It was the Dead Kennedys. They had got some money together, they were going to record their second single, 'Holiday In Cambodia', would I like to do it? Heck yeah, would I like to do it! That's how that went down. It was probably Biafra, because he and I by that time had something of a rapport. After that set I'm sure I went up to them and drooled, told them how great they were, that's always how it is if I fall in love with a band or a song. Maybe the sincerity of that wins bands over – I dunno."

"It was very difficult to find a recording engineer who was willing to throw away their '70s studio training," reflects Biafra, "and the whole '70s studio mentality, that everything needed to sound clean, muffled and mellow. Otherwise you'll never get to record the next Eagles or ELO! A lot of the people who made the early punk singles were learning how to record that kind of loud, fiery music by trial and error. A few, like Geza X, were applying what they learned from the straight studio world to make a fuller, nastier-sounding punk single than some of their peers. But a lot of the engineers actually fought the bands over the sound the bands wanted. Which makes it all the more ironic that some of the cartoon retro bands of the last ten years have set their guitars and amps in order to sound like badly-recorded late '70s punk singles, that weren't supposed to sound that way in the first place."

"It was crazy," Geza notes of the sessions. "It was Tewksbury Studio (in Richmond in the East Bay) where we did 'Holiday In Cambodia'. As with all other punk rock records, this was a semi-decent studio but it had some major equipment problems. What they had that was amazing, the guy who owned it [Dan Alexander] was kind of a fetishist for these antique tube microphones. They're the bomb, better than any other microphones at the time and revered to this day. Many of them come from immediately post-World War II. I was less acquainted with tube mics but I had repaired one in my Artist Recording Studio [where Geza had originally set up operations, close to The Masque] days. He was pulling them out in these drawers lined with red velvet. I was going, 'My God, these are like sex toys!' He brought out all these microphones including a particularly good-sounding vintage Neumann U47 [used extensively by George Martin in recording The Beatles]. So we got this U47 out – I was saying Biafra has a big manly voice, we want to get the fullness of that sound."

The microphones also had an impact on the record's overall acoustics. "We got two mics out," Geza continues. "We used one of them, a huge lollipop-like antique Sony, for the womb microphone on the giant reverberated echo-chambered guitar. I like it dry, but there was something about his [Ray's] guitar that needed a little extra something. I tight-mic'd it so it didn't get too much of the echo, then I got the far mic with this lollipop Sony. That was an experiment – I didn't know what that mic was going to sound like. And it sounded great on the womb mic of his amp. Then we also, I believe, had a couple of mics on the tom-toms, deluxe mics. Now in the control room, there was this big old Ampex MM1000 tape machine. If you've ever seen one, it looks like an industrial refrigerator up to the roof! And every channel you have to use lever switches on the actual channel. There's no remote to handle all that stuff – it's like an antique. It's a good-sounding machine – if you could get one that works, it would still be a good-sounding machine. So I learned how to use all that part of it, but the brakes weren't working. So for the entire record I was stopping the tape with my bare hands. If I would press stop, it would just go flying. I had to shuttle between rewind and fast forward until I could slow it down enough so I could stop it and grab it with my hands. That entire song could have just melted in the take – that's what's so funny about the whole thing. Because if the tape stretches you're screwed. I got burns on my hands from doing that!"

Watching the band in situ in the studio was as awe-inspiring as the Mabuhay performance. "Biafra was a crazy artist," Geza continues. "He had some practical real-world chops, but not like Ray. Ray was a real studious person. But when it came down to the studio stuff, Biafra had all of his lyric charts for both of us. He had everything underlined and circled where it needed to go, he was always there at the board helping me switch stuff in and out when I needed to do finger moves, cos there was no automation. There were several of us switching things on and off. There might have been several of us at the board when we mixed it, because it was too hard to do all the moves at once."

Another distinctive element of the sound on the single version of 'Holiday In Cambodia' was the percussion. "There's this crazy thing about the snare drum," notes Geza. "I tried to put some padding on the snare like I normally do, but he [Ted] had this unique head on it that I've never seen before. It looked like fibreglass, the kind you'd use on a surfboard. It was like a mesh. Anything I put on it was messing up the sound, so I think we just left it live. But that snare was some crazy cool thing because of the snare-hat. It had a 'ping'. I wasn't the best engineer yet – I was still fiddling around. We didn't have a lot of time to try things over and over, so some of it was – 'This sounds good on this. That sounds good on that.' We'd adjust it and modify it a bit, but there was a certain amount of luck that the record turned out sounding so good. A lot of it was Biafra's patience with me. I wanted to do stuff and he helped make that happen. And also his patience with all of the doubling. When we came to the original mix, we were switching stuff in and out on portions of the chorus. Biafra and I drew up a chart of where we doubled and quadrupled everything, then switched it in and out on the mix."

"I used two production masters," he continues, "I didn't just record the band. The stuff that was really hidden there was the doubling on all the guitars – in some places in the chorus the guitars were quadrupled, and the vocals on the chorus were also doubled or quadrupled. But it was punk rock, all those elements needed to be hidden, but that's one of the reasons it sounded so big. I had already learned a lot about those tricks. Ray, even though he had an Echoplex and all this other reverb, I took his guitar amplifier into an echo chamber, and I mic'd it close and far. So not only was it all his reverb and echo stuff, there was also a room echo that he was flatly insisting would not work, and it turned out to sound just incredible on the guitar. I want to put on the record too that I really respected Ray. He's a doll. He's always done such a good job on the business side [Geza maintains that of all those epochal records he produced in the late '70s, Dead Kennedys are the only band who have paid him]. I'm totally straight with him. He was always such a good business cat right from the beginning. He was the reason all of their stuff worked the way it did. He's a really competent person – an awesome guitar player. With me he's always been really laid-back and good-natured. Actually, I take that back a little bit. There was some conflict during the recording days. He did want to be a producer and there was tension between Ray and me and not Biafra and me. Biafra was going along with all of my ideas and Ray was kind of fighting them. So Biafra indulged me a little bit more than Ray did at the time. We were all still learning and experimenting. Afterwards my relationship with Ray became very good-natured, cos I saw what he was about and really respected him for it. Biafra was always a sort of bellicose and pompous person, and that was the beauty of his personality on stage and in interviews and everything."

The single endorsed and even enshrined Geza's growing reputation as sonic chronicler of West Coast punk. "It's funny, at the time the Dead Kennedys were so well known, and I got so much promotion value out of 'Holiday In Cambodia', still to this day everyone knows I did that. I only did parts of the other records where they would have one person recording the music tracks because – probably because Ray preferred it. That was Thom Wilson [producer of *Plastic Surgery Disasters*] who was doing some great records at the time, no complaints there. Then having me do the vocals with Biafra, which is a big job but a very fun job. An intense guy, but he didn't like working with anyone but me. We had a really good bond there."

For Ted's part, he again prefers the single version every time. "I always liked 'Holiday In Cambodia', but not the version so much that's on *Fresh Fruit*." Jello agrees. "The single version sends more chills down my spine. Some of that was the Geza X factor, too." Ray is not convinced. "It's interesting that Biafra and Ted both loved the singles more. And those were the ones that I mixed! [Biafra disputes Ray's right to take overarching credit for either single's mix]. I actually mixed them [the two sides of the single, 'Holiday In Cambodia' and 'Police Truck'] by myself. Nobody was there. What happened was that Geza was mixing them, and nobody liked them, and then I said, let me go mix them. I brought them back, and the band chose two of those over the Geza ones. But I don't want to cut down Geza. I wanted the sound to be in front of the speakers rather than behind the speakers. I wanted it to sound like the band was in the room with you."

"Yeah," confirms Geza, "he [Ray] mixed it. I did a mix, and when they played it in other rooms it didn't have enough bass in it, so he went back and remixed it himself. That's fine. I recall that the first mix did not have enough bass in it. And he was right, when we went and checked it out, it did not have enough bass. In those days, that was a chronic mix problem of mine, so that wouldn't have been an exaggeration. It does seem to me that he went and mixed it himself after that, cos I don't recall going back and doing anything like that. And I do vaguely recall being OK with it, because it sounded like it was supposed to – he kept it exactly the way it sounded."

'Holiday In Cambodia' saw 3,000 copies pressed in America on Optional, who had picked up the rights to its predecessor, before it was re-released on Faulty Products. The 'indie' distribution arm of IRS, run by Miles Copeland, Faulty was formed when A&M's Jerry Moss, a yachting buddy of Ted Kennedy, refused to distribute material by the band because of their name. In the UK, it would bear the Cherry Red imprint on release in May 1980. The same agreements would eventually extend to the release of the band's debut album, too (although, significantly, the US release followed its UK counterpart by four months in January 1981). If there has ever been a more fully-formed, exhilarating punk single than 'Holiday In Cambodia', your correspondent has yet to hear it. "If the other guys had pushed as hard as I did," laments Biafra, "and we kept coming up with band-written songs like 'Holiday In Cambodia', instead of me writing most of the music, how good a band would we have been? We were a pretty good band, but we could have been an *even better* band."

Overleaf above left: Slip and Slide Jello 1978. Jello Biafra at the Mabuhay. (Photograph by Ruby Ray)
Overleaf below left: Jello Swim 1978. On floor of the grimy Mabuhay stage. (Photograph by Ruby Ray)

NEW WAVE TURNS SILVER

Mabuhay Gardens

Mon., Oct. 29,1979

8 p.m. Buffet

8:30 p.m. Music

443 Broadway

$4.00 Donation

DeadKennedys
Jim Carroll
SS I
COR YAIRS
FLESHAPOIDS
TIMES 5

BENEFIT For

Carol Ruth Silver

District Attorney

92

CHERRY 13....DEAD KENNEDYS/HOLIDAY IN CAMBODIA b/w POLICE TRUCK......

..P & C 1980 CHERRY RED RECORDS,199 KINGSTON ROAD,LONDON S.W.19

HOLIDAY IN CAMBODIA TAKEN FROM FORTHCOMING DEAD KENNEDYS ALBUM A RED 10.....

...DISTRIBUTION BY SPARTAN,LONDON ROAD,WEMBLEY,MIDDLESEX 9AH 7HQ

Jello Biafra/vocals...
..E.B.Ray/guitars.....
Klaus Flouride/bass,vocals
Bruce Slesinger/drums..
Produced by GezaX & Dead
Kennedys......Mixed by
R.Pepperell... = +++++++

design/annie horwood

94

HOLIDAY IN CAMBODIA

DEAD KENNEDYS

HOLIDAY IN CAMBODIA

DEAD KENNEDYS

POLICE TRUCK

CHERRY 13

....JELLO BIAFRA/VOCALS.....E.B. RAY/GUITARS.....

....KLAUS FLOURIDE/BASS:VOCALS.....BRUCE SLESINGER/DRUMS...

....PRODUCED BY GEZA X & DEAD KENNEDYS.....MIXED BY R.PEPPERELL......

....(P)&(C) 1980 CHERRY RED RECORDS,53 KENSINGTON GARDENS SQUARE, LONDON W2 4BA...

...DISTRIBUTED BY PINNACLE RECORDS, ELECTRON HOUSE, CRAY ROAD, ORPINGTON, KENT....

'Holiday in Cambodia' appears on Dead Kennedys album 'Fresh Fruit for Rotting Vegetables' B RED 10...

95

A frightening communication gap . . .

POLICE TRUCK (w-Biafra/m-Biafra,Ray)

Tonight's the night that we got the truck
We're goin downtown Gonna beat up drunks
Your turn to drive I'll bring the beer
It's the late late shift No one to fear
AND RIDE, RIDE HOW WE RIDE
WE RIDE, LOWRIDE
It's roundup time Where the good whores meet
Gonna drag one screaming Off the street
AND RIDE, RIDE HOW WE RIDE
Got a black uniform And a silver badge
Playin' cops for real/Playin' cops for pay
LET'S RIDE, LOWRIDE

Pull down your dress Here's a kick in the ass
Let's beat you blue 'Til you shit in your pants
Don't move, child Got a big black stick
There's six of us, babe So suck on my dick
AND RIDE, RIDE HOW WE RIDE
LET'S RIDE, LOWRIDE
The left newspapers Might whine a bit
But the guys at the station They don't give a shit
Dispatch calls 'Are you doin' something wicked?
No siree, Jack, We're just givin' tickets
AS WE RIDE, RIDE, HOW WE RIDE (3)
LET'S RIDE, LOWRIDE

(c) DECAY MUSIC (BMI)

Pages 92-93: 'Holiday In Cambodia' / 'Police Truck' – US release 1980 (Optional Music / Faulty Products)
Previous pages: 'Holiday In Cambodia' / 'Police Truck' – UK release 1980 first + second pressing (Cherry Red)
Previous pages: 'Holiday In Cambodia' / 'Police Truck' – Label, Italian release 1981 (Ariston)
Above: Lyric Insert – US release 1980 (Optional Music)
Right: 'Holiday In Cambodia' / 'Police Truck' – Label, French release 1980 (Cherry Red)
Far right: 'Holiday In Cambodia' / 'Police Truck' – Label, Australian release 1980 first pressing (Missing Link)

HOLIDAY IN CAMBODIA
(w-Biafra/m-Biafra,Ray,Fluoride,Slesinger)

So you been to school For a year or two
And you know you've seen it all
In daddy's car Thinkin' you'll go far
Back east your type don't crawl
Play ethnicky jazz To parade your snazz
On your five grand stereo
Braggin that you know How the niggers feel cold
And the slums got so much soul
It's time to taste what you most fear
Right Guard will not help you here
Brace yourself, my dear
IT'S A HOLIDAY IN CAMBODIA
IT'S TOUGH, KID, BUT IT'S LIFE
IT'S A HOLIDAY IN CAMBODIA
DON'T FORGET TO PACK A WIFE
You're a star-belly sneech You suck like a leech
You want everyone to act like you
Kiss ass while you bitch So you can get rich
But your boss gets richer off you
Well you'll work harder With a gun in your back
For a bowl of rice a day
Slave for soldiers Til you starve
Then your head is skewered on a stake
Now you can go where people are one
Now you can go where they get things done
What you need, my son.....
IS A HOLIDAY IN CAMBODIA
WHERE PEOPLE DRESS IN BLACK
A HOLIDAY IN CAMBODIA
WHERE YOU'LL KISS ASS OR CRACK
(chant) POL POT/POL POT/POL POT/POL POT/etc.
And it's a HOLIDAY IN CAMBODIA
WHERE YOU'LL DO WHAT YOU'RE TOLD
A HOLIDAY IN CAMBODIA
WHERE THE SLUMS GOT SO MUCH SOUL

(c) 1979 DECAY MUSIC (BMI)

Band: 70 Lundys Ln, SF CA 94110
Distribution: Systematic, 729 Heinz, Berkeley CA 94710
415/845/3352

Above: 'Holiday In Cambodia' / 'Police Truck' – Australian release 1980 second pressing (Missing Link)

Above: 'Holiday In Cambodia' / 'Police Truck' – Jukebox card insert

Right: Portion of a collage by John Yates from the booklet included with the Dead Kennedys album *Give Me Convenience Or Give Me Death*

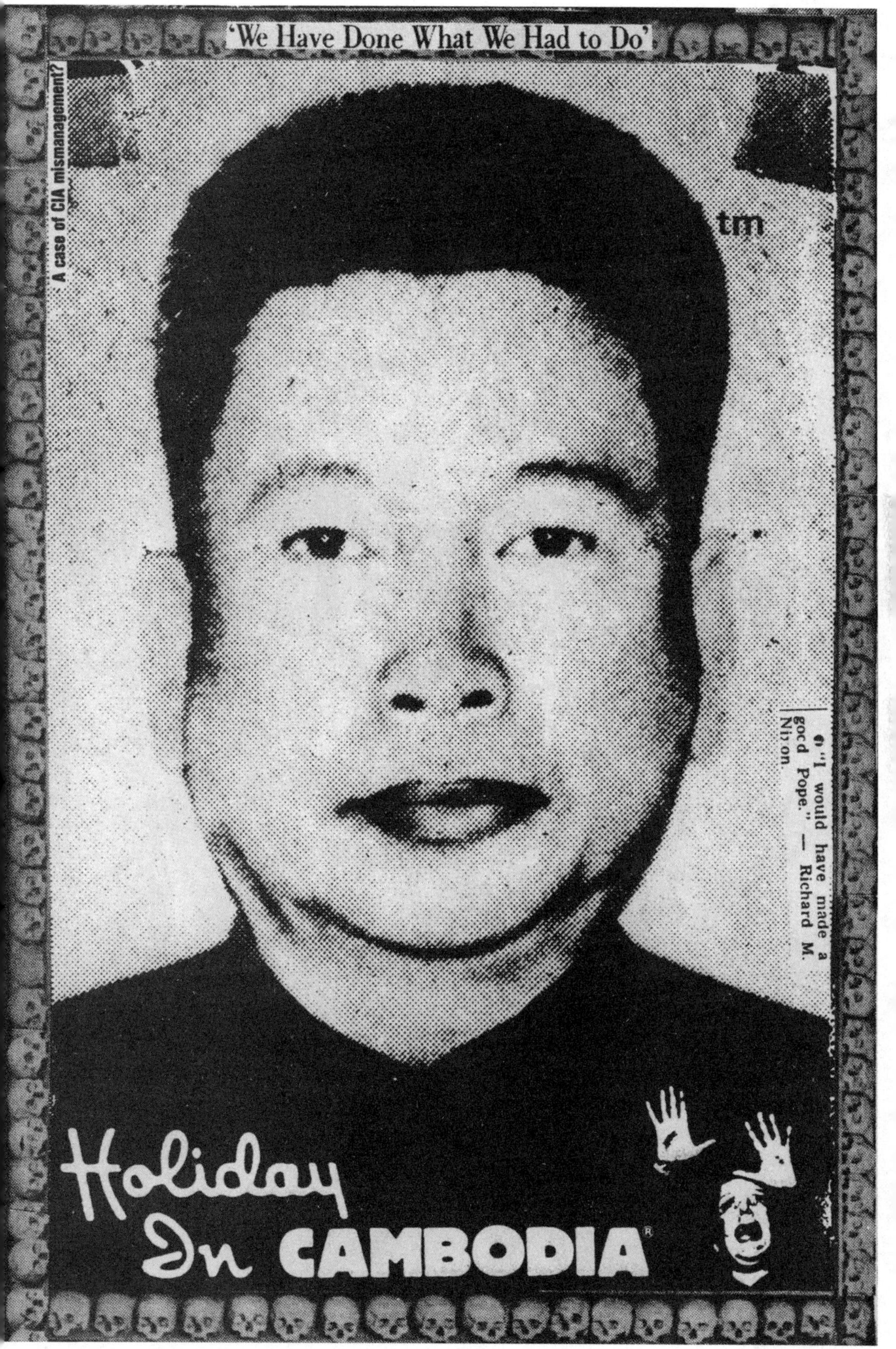
'We Have Done What We Had to Do'
A case of CIA mismanagement?
tm
"I would have made a good Pope." — Richard M. Nixon.
Holiday In CAMBODIA®

out that our government dumped
the stuff, that's different.

ings

the tWits PTA and the DiPShits

NOW AT THE ORB
$3.00 AT THE DOOR

Copyright 1939

Chapter 6

Efficiency and Progress
Is Ours Once More

Music, in performance, is a type of sculpture.
The air in the performance is sculpted into something.
(Frank Zappa)

Fresh Fruit For Rotting Vegetables was recorded at Mobius Music in San Francisco. "Iain and I both took a chance," reflects Bill Gilliam, "by sending the money over to make the album to a San Francisco band who could have shoved it all up their nose." As it was, there was more danger that the drink/drug-free Biafra would have spent it on his ever-expanding record collection. They need not have worried. The sessions were disciplined and well ordered. "I suppose I'm quite trusting by nature," McNay says. "I was confident it would all be OK."

The band chose Oliver DiCicco's studio in Noe Valley, which had just been converted to 16-track, and is affectionately recalled as a 'shoebox', with the band set up in one central, carpeted room with no isolation booths. The month-long sessions generally took place at night owing to Klaus's day job, with roughly a week each for basic tracks, overdubs, backing vocals and keyboard and horn overdubs and finally mixing. "There was carpet on the floor, fibreglass panels on the walls with burlap on them and then bare sheetrock," DiCicco recalled to Heather Johnson in 2005. "It was a small room and isolation was difficult to achieve. It was probably as bare bones of a recording as you could do. It wasn't fancy, but it was going to two-inch 16-track, so there was plenty of tape real estate to put sound on. Tape hiss wasn't a problem, because the sound never stopped!" As Ted confirms, "It was a very nice little studio in San Francisco. A very comfortable atmosphere."

As DiCicco intimates, the whole sound of the album can be attributed to a variety of enhancements but just as crucially, restraints; his main difficulty was the wall of sound the band created and his difficulty in distinguishing component elements as a result. Ray used a DOD Overdrive pre-amp for the sessions, the Fender Super Reverb, and his trusty Echoplex – an echo chamber frequently employed in

Left: Blur 1978. Biafra was seldom still when onstage. (Photograph by Ruby Ray)

the '60s to produce UFO-type effects on sci-fi serials. He bought one after listening to Scotty Moore using one on 'Mystery Train'. Biafra had gravitated to using higher quality Neumann U47 microphones at the suggestion of Geza X to add lustre to his vocals; DiCicco overseeing the final mix on his Ampex 351 two-track. According to DiCicco, "nothing was fast enough or loud enough" for Biafra, who would monitor the mixes in an upstairs lounge where a set of basic speakers gave him a chance to approximate how the recordings might actually sound on vinyl.

"Cherry Red gave us $10,000," Ray recalls, "and I suggested to the band we use $6,000, and we get $1,000 each, because that's probably the last money we'd see! So we did it for $6,000. I'd been reading recording books and subscribed to the magazines back in the day. And they said the way to maximise your studio time is pre-production. And that's when you really know what you're going to do, it's all mapped out. You have this much time to do the basics, recording the bass and drums, then this much time for guitar overdubs, this much time for lead and background vocals. This much time for the fancy stuff like keyboards and horns and then this much time for mixing. It was all planned out. People don't realise in music, you read about these musicians on MTV, and it all looks like fun and games. But 99% perspiration, 1% inspiration."

"We were meticulous," confirms Biafra. "We were never – and I have never been – fast in the studio. 'California Über Alles', just a goddamn single, took a month. But the results speak for themselves. The rest of the band would really get down on me for being too picky, or not looking at my watch, like Ray always did, perhaps because I didn't own one at the time. My feeling about this was, it wasn't just an attempt to document what we played at our live shows. I felt as a record collector and a fan, that these versions of the songs are the ones that everyone is going to hear five, ten, fifty years from now. So as far as I was concerned, they damn well better be the best version of the song we ever played. That was the standard I tried to maintain. How many arguments it took!"

Biafra had wanted Geza X to produce the album, based on how well 'Cambodia' had turned out. "The other guys shot that idea down," he says. "So we realised, we're going to have to do it ourselves and hope for the best." Ted recalls how the sessions panned out. "Ray, Klaus and I were in there first. We laid down three or four tracks for songs, and we thought they were pretty good tracks. And this was before Biafra showed up. Biafra came in and dismissed them all and said we've got to do them faster or something. We were a little put off by it, but I guess it turned out OK. There was probably a little time wasted, but overall it was pretty organised, the whole session.

Most of the songs were so well rehearsed; we were playing so many shows at the time and also rehearsing quite a bit. We had most of the stuff down before we ever got into the studio. There was some overdubbing, but the basic tracks were done in one or two takes."

Increasing confidence drawn from their live shows meant they were pumped for the occasion. "Yeah, it was exciting for me," Ted continues. "'California' was the first time I'd been in a recording studio, so you had that out of the way, so to speak. You weren't so much in awe of being in a studio for the first time. It was kind of fun. Whether or not I knew what I wanted to do with the sound, I had an idea of what I wanted my own drums to sound like, but it was Ray and Biafra who did more of the production of it."

"There's several different takes of each of those songs as far as I remember," recalls Biafra. "I wound up being the one that always chose which takes or mix to use. With 'In-Sight' we had a faster one that Ray thought was better, but I liked the one we actually used, because I thought the song was more locked in and captured better." ['In-Sight' wasn't included on the album itself, but was the one additional song recorded at the sessions and later became the b-side to the single version of 'Kill The Poor'.]

"Oliver had never worked on this type of music," Biafra continues. "His main forte before us was people who became big new age musicians. One was Andy Narrell, another one was Alex Di Grassi. It's important, because Oliver was so far in another field, yet he pulled this off. Unlike a lot of established engineers of the day, he was game to try to get the kind of sound we wanted. I would say he was mostly responsible, then Ray was with him in the console room. I was upstairs where there was another set of speakers. I would just stay out of earshot while Oliver tinkered with the various instruments. Then when he had a mix, he'd play it into those other speakers, and I'd make notes and come back in and decide what to do from there. I use that procedure to this day. I try to stay completely out of earshot of the engineer and let him do his job until he's got something worked up. Otherwise I could bitch and moan about the snare drum for six hours. Then, once I get a perfect snare drum, everything else would sound terrible. So I learned to stay away from that part of the process. To this day, I stay out of the room until the engineer thinks he's got something. Then I do the fine-tuning from there, or occasionally just rip it all down and try something else."

It's fair to say Biafra and Ray don't see eye-to-eye on the production credits. "On the record, the problem is [that] I didn't have enough control over the mix," states Ray. "Biafra was coming in, sticking his nose in. I was looking back, thinking it would have been better if we'd kicked him out of the room and did the mixes and said, 'Here!' Biafra says Oliver oversaw the production. Actually, it was Oliver and me. I have all the EQ sheets, they're 90% my handwriting. I have the overdub sheets in my handwriting. I can prove it! The fact that Biafra has forgotten about it is not my problem. That was recorded on 16 tracks. So 16 channels, basically duplicates of each other, but one for the bass, the guitar, the voices and different drums. You need to keep track of that on an intellectual level, where things are, how they're being routed and blended together. I didn't realise it at the time, but I'm good at song arranging – making it go someplace. You don't wanna stay in one place too long, you want to keep the person's ears interested."

Producer status was eventually given to DiCicco's cat, Norm. "Oliver had two cats, Norm and Motto," Biafra continues. "But Norm was by far the friendlier! I hadn't been around a cat since I left home, so I was happy to have Norm's company and unwavering support. Even if he was sleeping in the middle of the mixing board when Oliver needed to get at some of the knobs. Obviously Norm was the producer. To this day, I get enquiries from bands wondering if I can put them in touch with Norm, so he can produce their album. But unfortunately, like Joe Meek before him, I'm afraid he's passed on."

Fresh Fruit emphatically sustained the songwriting pedigree of both singles. None of the fourteen tracks lacked a unique musical or lyrical hook. At times the humour is frantic and mischievous ('Stealing People's Mail', the cover of 'Viva Las Vegas'), at other times chilling and antagonistic ('I Kill Children', 'Funland At The Beach' and 'Ill In The Head'). Biafra's critics have targeted the last subset as being particularly sinister. But it was his customised shock therapy in his personal crusade for rejection of American moral platitudes. "I wasn't sitting out and planning ahead of time to break this or that taboo," he says. "I was just trying to say things that I thought needed to be said. Once I knew I could write songs and compose music and write lyrics, and realised that I was pretty good at it, there was no stopping me. So my standard has always been that every single one of my songs has to be something that I, the picky fan, would like to listen to, over and over again. I'd been through so many years of growing up on rock 'n' roll and thinking that most of the lyrics were so stupid. That's partly what made punk such a breath of fresh air. The lyrics were volatile, topical. There was a real pressure to be intelligent, especially in San Francisco." And that applied to the music, too. "Everybody in DKs had this competitive edge," notes Ray. "We want to write a better song than *that* band. We all had that in common.

Fortunately we had the talent to do so. Some people just have the ego, and ego with no talent . . ."

It seems impossible that anyone could eavesdrop, say, 'Funland At The Beach', and its chorus of "Crushed little kids adorn the boardwalk" and not smirk at its glorious profanity. But they did. "What I was trying to do with the music was try to make a Dead Kennedys song that had the fire of The Sonics," Biafra recalls. "But what I had for lyrics at the time was a long, free-verse poem with much more detail in it, called 'Funland At The Beach'. Then I had to chop it down to turn it into a Sonics-inspired punk rock song. Originally, when we were trying to mix that, it came out sounding kinda blurry, and the guitar was undefined. I can't remember which one of us came up with the idea, but it was suggested Ray add another track of guitar where he played this low E-string, single-string twang like Duane Eddy. Then we kinda 'multed' that down in the mix, where you can't really hear the Duane Eddy guitar, but the riff is much more clearly defined."

But one lyric would win the moral outrage sweepstakes by several lengths. "What I got most shit for over the years was 'I Kill Children'," Biafra confirms. "The premise of the song was, why does America have so many more mass murderers and serial killers than other countries? Supposedly, America has had more serial killers than all of the countries in the history of the world combined. Why? That's what the bridge of the song tries to answer. Ironically, the people who objected to that song most deeply were the religious right in the United States and the early British Crass punks. They thought it was too violent, and too mindlessly blood-splattered. Then again, Alice Cooper is a part of my being too! I just tried to make the horror scenes something out of real life, instead of vampires and monsters."

'Kill The Poor' opened the album, anchored by peppy, across-the-beat drumming from Ted. "One of the things that Ted did," recalls Klaus, "he would change things up all the time. As much as we would speed up, he would like to change up the beat sometimes. That would sometimes throw Biafra a little bit. It became a sticking point between them. It was Ted's experimentation. Whereas Biafra in performance, he basically wanted to know where it was going. As a result of stuff like that, that's how 'Kill The Poor' ended up being the disco thing on the *Deaf Club* album, for instance."

Indeed, the version of the song from that March 1979 show, which took place at the eponymous underground club in the Mission District of San Francisco and was released retrospectively in 2004, has him doing just that, though it sounds more like jazz-funk to these ears. "Bruce [aka Ted] is a snap-tight drummer," continues Klaus.

"'Kill The Poor' – the intro is a standard doo-wop progression, then it cuts into your standard Sex Pistols-type punk stuff, except faster." In fact, the song was originally intended as a pastiche of the Ramones' 'You're Gonna Kill That Girl'. Quite a few people did spot the similarity in the chorus, on which Biafra's whooping enunciation of 'tonight' had more oscillations than a Dickie Nixon lie-detector, but according to the singer were "a nod to Buddy Holly".

'Kill The Poor', which mock-worshipped the neutron bomb and its 'clean' dispatch of what Scrooge once called 'the excess population', was an excellent example of Biafra's penchant for twists on standard punk rhetoric. Its restrained hysteria was reminiscent of Jonathan Swift's satirical *A Modest Proposal for Preventing the Children of Poor People in Ireland from Being a Burden to Their Parents or Country*, which proposed a leavening of economic blight by the destitute selling their children as food for the rich. It wasn't, on the surface, a protest song loaded with imperatives, the common denominator among punk bands addressing the topic. "There's all kinds of anti-nuclear songs coming out," Biafra confirms, "especially from older Californian hippy bands and British punk bands from a different perspective. So why not tap into my method acting brain and do a song coming from the *military's* point of view? Or the Pentagon Madmens' point of view? It will make it that much more evil. That was how 'Kill The Poor' was born."[9]

Not everyone would prove fully conversant in Biafra's brand of sarcasm, however. At one Brooklyn gig a girl, exploring the farthest reaches of literalism, rushed up to him in the dressing room exclaiming: 'Awright! Kill the poor!' Cherry Red's German licensee did not include the lyric sheet with the album as a cost-cutting measure, and as a result, claims Biafra, some "assumed it was an anthem for open season on Turks. I straightened that out from the stage right away." In fact, and for obvious reasons, it was 'California Über Alles' that would create most problems in Germany. The band later hired, by coincidence rather than planning, a Turkish promoter for their Berlin shows in a move falsely portrayed as a 'scam' by racist German newspapers. 'Kill The Poor' had already caused a degree of more local difficulty. "One of the reasons we had to move out of our garage," confirms Ray, "apart from getting a drummer, the rehearsal that set the neighbours off to get the police was learning the song 'Kill The Poor'. I think it was the repetition of 'Kill Kill Kill Kill' that did it."

The band's sound had stretched prior to the sessions. "By the time the album was recorded," notes Klaus, "there had been an organic thing; it germinated. We played around with all sorts of different permutations of how the songs could be in practice, going over and over the stuff. That's how the songs all became where they are, someone would come in with an idea. Or between songs we'd jam on something, me and Ray, Bruce would kick in, and Biafra would put on the tape recorder and come back later with some lyrics to the section we'd played, and the song would grow out of that. It was very organic and it took a while to come up with a 38-minute album. I don't think there was anything that was filler on that record. That was something that was cool about it."

"One of the things that is a source of that," Ray points out, "was that the people in the band all listened to different kinds of music. We had punk rock in common, but Klaus had a big 78 RPM library of '30s jazz, and he also had the wacky Spike Jones comedy stuff. Biafra had a lot of garage rock stuff. 6025 was listening to more *avant garde* stuff like Captain Beefheart. This is what makes a band great, to my mind, compared to a solo artist. You have different musicians who are talented, they bring in different viewpoints and you mush them all together and come out with something new. That's kind of how rock 'n' roll originated, country, blues, gospel, jazz, a hybrid thing."

A nice, and common, idea in theory, but rarely does it work so well in practice. "Well, the basic thing is," states Ray, "we rock out! In the *New Yorker*, there used to be a jazz critic, Whitney Balliett. He was a really, really good writer. Even if you didn't like the person he was talking about, you'd just read him for the writing. His bottom line was whether the jazz musician *swung* or not. And it's like that with a rock 'n' roll band, whether the energy is there."

One of the most enjoyable aspects of *Fresh Fruit* is its readiness to defy listeners' expectations, delighting in finding a route out of a song just when you may have got a handle on the structure. People picked up on the humour in the lyrics immediately. But much of that wit is also embodied in the music. "Yeah," confirms Ray, "there's definitely musical jokes in there. It's not on the record, but recorded at a similar time, was 'Police Truck'. Right before the solo starts, Klaus and I do the *Batman* theme."

'Police Truck' is also a favourite with Ted, who believes the essence of the performances on the album was due to live groundwork. "We played a lot live, so there's a certain energy when you play live. The hardest part with that, and a lot of bands have the same problem, is capturing that raw, live energy in a recording studio. Some days were better than others, just in terms of the times when we recorded, whether or not it was in the morning or later in the day. It's difficult to capture that live, raw feeling and excitement that you get on stage. There's an adrenaline rush you get when there's an audience there, participating. The type of music we were playing required some of that stimulant. I think we did the best we could at the time." According to

Biafra, 'Police Truck' was one of "only three songs I wrote in thirty minutes or less all in one go. 'Nazi Punks Fuck Off' and 'Voted Off The Island' were the others. Ray added cool trademark guitar stuff later so yes, he earned a co-writing credit."

'Let's Lynch The Landlord' was partly inspired by Klaus and Biafra's experience of rented accommodation, although stories that did the rounds about the latter gaining revenge against the titular villain by rearing a colony of mice in the building's basement are "entirely fictional", he states. Well, that's his own fault for advancing the idea in an interview with John Tobler at *Zig Zag*, in which he related the tale of charging overdue plumbing repairs against his rent and encountering a very large and surly gentleman knocking on his door as a result. "It still has the same landlady," he says now. "If she's still alive, she could sue us for slander! If you really want to expand on that, you can say that it appears to have had *very few repairs* to this day."

The song proved to be the most difficult to pin down. Nobody was entirely sure why. "Eventually we all agreed that Bruce needed to re-cut his kick drum to 'Let's Lynch The Landlord' and use something a little more simple," Biafra continues. "You could almost see the steam coming out of his ears as he sat in the studio with nothing but his kick drum just tapping away. But it helped the song. 'Let's Lynch The Landlord' was a song you should be able to dance to, and we couldn't figure out why it wasn't quite doing what it was supposed to. Then Oliver took me into the console room and said, 'Listen to this kick drum. It's going to be a problem in the mix.' So then we had Bruce redo it. Oliver realised pretty early on who was the most emotionally involved in the album, and he and I hit it off pretty well."

'Chemical Warfare' revelled in a country club massacre fantasy. Cold War paranoia later ensured that the prospect of biological extermination become another favoured topic within the punk canon. But no songs of similar title employed images of nerve gas rolling through golf greens and dry martinis crashing to the floor as the moneyed and complacent choke to death. None, to my certain knowledge, threw in a passable impression of an oompah band either. "Ah, the waltz," Biafra recalls. "That came from my love of Sparks. I loved the wicked humour of Frank Zappa, and the dry but really demented Sparks' lyrics on *Kimono My House*, *Propaganda* and especially *Indiscreet*. I suppose the Mael brothers were a bigger influence on my own writing style than anyone else." In fact, the quote on the run-out groove of early pressings of the album, 'Well?? Who ARE The Brain Police???' drew its provenance from a song by Zappa's Mothers of Invention.

The 'choke' scene featured the massed ranks of the Rocky Mountain Arsenal Choir, named after the infamous chemical weapons facility. "We just had a mass of people in there," Klaus remembers. "I'm not sure if we did it all in one take, or if Oliver had us do it two or three times through. We had a bunch of people there, some of them ended up being in Flipper." Indeed, Will Shatter, formerly of Negative Trend and latterly Flipper, was one contributor, alongside journalist (and occasional Tubes lyricist) Michael Snyder, the band's then manager Chi Chi, Dirk Dirksen and Ninotchka. The latter, aka Therese Soder of punk band The Situations, would later marry Biafra. In a graveyard. I put it to her former husband that the song neatly anticipates America's current fallacy or obsession with 'homeland security'. "You said it, I didn't. But the illusion of homeland security, the fallacy, whatever you want to call it – that's a good way of describing 'Chemical Warfare'."

It was written "from the point of view of how easy it would be to break into the Rocky Mountain Arsenal in Colorado and steal nerve gas and drop it on a nearby golf course," Biafra continues. "No other songs approached the subject of biological weapons that way. In a way it's a current way of thinking about it. It wouldn't necessarily be a deranged prankster, it could be a very methodical al-Qaida-type terrorist. The Bush administration had all kinds of bells and whistles to terrify airline passengers and lock up people of Mid-Eastern descent and put them in jail without trial, but our military weapons storage sites and nuclear power plants are largely unprotected, as are our shipping lanes. Hardly any of the cargo that comes off ships into our ports is ever inspected. You could just smuggle Osama Bin Laden in one of those containers, you could smuggle in a big-ass surface to air missile. Osama could be driving in a cab in New York right now, and nobody would know." These comments were made, of course, prior to Obama's 'decisive action' to eliminate the hirsute enemy of peace, democracy and the American Way. The Rocky Mountain Arsenal, meanwhile, has finally been cleaned up and designated a nature sanctuary.

As well as 'Holiday In Cambodia', which in album form featured an extended intro that somehow managed to replicate the sound of human screaming, Ray employed his Echoplex on other songs like 'Drug Me' and several solos, including 'Let's Lynch The Landlord'. Improbably, his incredible sheet treble sound on the album was cultivated on ultra-low-budget equipment. "I played a Japanese pawnshop Telecaster copy guitar, which I purchased for $100. I had added Seymour Duncan pickups, a humbucker at the bridge and a Strat style for the neck, and a Schecter bridge. I still have it and it definitely has a unique sound."

'Your Emotions', with a lyric by Ray, owed a direct debt to the band's San Francisco punk forefathers. "The bass part for that," explains Klaus, "there's a part where it goes into the chorus and I do this one-five-one-five thing, which I saw from the Avengers. The Avengers pre-dated us, they were one of the bands I really liked watching. They were one of the bands that made me decide I wanted to get into a punk band. The bass player is Jimmy Wilsey, who ended up playing guitar for Chris Isaak. At the time, back in '77/'78, he was playing this astoundingly aggressive bass. He had this one part that went really fast, and I thought, OK, I'm going to put that in *this* thing. Some of it, again, is real old influences. Some are influences that had come in the last year. You borrow. You steal. Amateurs borrow, professionals steal."

'Forward To Death', a brutal, nihilistic thrash, was written by the departed 6025, though on the finished album he only actually played on 'Ill In The Head', adding overdubs. "6025 wanted to do more *avant garde* stuff," says Ray. "He thought we were too mainstream and poppy! Although 6025 brought in 'Forward To Death', it really was a band effort. People have a hard time knowing how band dynamics work in a musical situation. That one he brought in, but that's straight-ahead punk rock, The chord pattern – it wouldn't matter who played that. But after the first verse, I do some little single line things. Someone described it as a wall of sound with graffiti on it. So there are graffiti parts in there, if you listen. Those were probably just made up in practice, or maybe at a show. When you play for an audience, the song changes a bit." According to Ted, "through rehearsals and jamming we all figured out on our own what was the best. There were suggestions from other members of the band, why don't you try this, or that, so it was a somewhat collaborative effort on most of the songs. But overall every person was responsible for coming up with their own part or how they would play".

'Ill In The Head' was "much more angular," according to Ray. "We would try to make it more digestible for punk rock people, I guess." It still retains, however, several separate sections and time signatures, ostensibly moving from a thirteen-eight to eleven-eight structure. Both traits are exceedingly uncommon in Western musical composition (though the Grateful Dead, Van der Graaf Generator, Caravan and other prog-rock groups experimented with the latter) but more prominent in Turkish and Romany traditions. "It would have had even more parts if we hadn't edited it!" Ray laughs. "One of the parts of the creative process is editing. What you take out can make what's left sound better." But then, as Klaus notes, "All the songs, everyone has a little bit that they bring in. 'Ill In The Head' was basically a 6025 song. But the thing that was purely his on that song was the ending, in terms of what the guitars are playing. My bass part – he didn't tell me what to play, but the idea of those three little sections at the end was 6025's. It was a strange thing for us to learn, but he put it down. Then I came up with the idea of playing the three against the four on the bass.

6025 wanted us to play something like eleven-eight at the end for part of it. There are things like that put in there totally to throw someone."

The song had stemmed from Biafra handing Carlos a set of lyrics without music, the only time, he maintains, he did that in the band. "I just handed it to Carlos and let him play around with the words and come up with some music from it. I largely stepped back from writing the music when he was in the band, because he seemed to be coming up with more surprises more quickly, and I lost confidence for a while. 'Chemical Warfare' was the first song I brought in after he left the band. Years later he showed me a completely different version of the words to 'Ill In The Head' that he said I had handed him first. It turned out that the ones he had were better, but by then the album was out, so it was a little late."

Carlos would subsequently work with Residents collaborator Snakefinger (he appears in the video to 'The Man In The Dark Sedan'). Rumours abound about the DKs' second guitarist's subsequent mental frailty. He is still, apparently, finishing his Christian punk rock opera. "He had been deeply religious in high school," recalls Biafra, "then chucked religion when he was in Dead Kennedys. Thus the 'Religious Vomit' song he wrote [which the band would record for *In God We Trust, Inc.*]. Later he went back to religion and told me, at one point, he wanted to be the Captain Beefheart of gospel music." His last brush with notoriety came in April 1993 when he attended a show at the Gilman Street punk venue and was so outraged by the lewd acts performed by Marian Anderson of InSaints, involving lesbian dominatrix sessions, that he called the police. Coverage of the event made reference to fist-fucking and bananas, which may or may not have taken place, but Biafra believes "two women kissing would have been enough for Carlos". It led to his former band-mates answering a slew of awkward questions about why a former Dead Kennedy would become an overnight prude and police informant.

"He left," confirms Ray, "but they were good songs, and we'd been playing them, and added our own twist to them to keep them. In 'Ill In The Head' there's a two-guitar harmony part, so we asked him to come in to play his part. After he left the band, I don't think we played that live anymore. It needs two interlocking guitar parts. Perhaps I could have got a double-neck guitar!" Biafra's recall is different. "'Ill In The Head' was in our repertoire all the way to the end, 'Drug Me' too. One statement to their musicianship is that we *always* knew all our songs. So our sets changed nightly. If I called out 'Drug Me' on the spur of the moment, we could play it. The guitar part in between the verse-vocal lines of 'Ill In The Head' is Carlos playing the part he wrote for Ray *backwards*. Carlos was very proud of that."

"He wanted to go in a more prog-rock direction than the other guys in the band," Biafra continues. "He even, at one point, asked me if I would take up flute, because that's what Ian Anderson played with Jethro Tull. He hadn't cut the cord with the excesses of '70s rock nearly as much as the rest of the band! I think he may have been the most brilliant musician we ever had in the band. He could play anything. He even got behind the drum set to show Bruce how he wanted him to play the ending in 'Ill In The Head', and he played it perfectly! He was a musical genius."

"Why can't Biafra say *that* about Klaus and me?" demands Ray, inadvertently coughing up one huge emotional fur ball. "It would be nice if he said something nice about my unique guitar-playing. I'm going to cry here!" He's only half-joking, too. Without getting into the grist of songwriting dues, Biafra, due to other factors, has always been circumspect about crediting the excellence of Ray and Klaus's musical contributions to Dead Kennedys. Ray *is* indisputably a great guitar player, with an incredibly varied palette and distinctive sound. Klaus too has a highly individual touch; his bass lines intractably harmonious, regardless of the brutality of the musical landscape, while his talent for arranging is a comparatively unacknowledged facet of *Fresh Fruit*.[10]

In retaining 6025's songwriting contributions to the band, it's important to note that the eventual track selection was deliberately time-sealed. "By the time we made *Fresh Fruit*," says Biafra, "I guess we had a feeling we might be around for a while. We didn't have to shoot our wad all on one album. We had 'Bleed For Me' and maybe even 'Moon Over Marin' by then, and then some of the songs that wound up on [subsequent mini-album] *In God We Trust, Inc.*. But I had a strong feeling that we shouldn't just drop the early, simpler punk songs, and go into what turned into *Plastic Surgery Disasters*, to capture us right then in the moment. I thought it was important to document everything, step by step. Thus we didn't record 'Bleed For Me', but we did record songs like 'Your Emotions' or 'Ill In The Head' that we weren't really playing much anymore. I wound up choosing the final mixes and track order. I figured it out the same way I figure out track orders today – just cruise around in my car, listening to one until it works." Ray, unsurprisingly enough, disputes that Biafra chose the running order. "There's a whole bunch of notes in my handwriting. What happened was – we picked four orders and put them in a hat. And everybody voted on it." And Biafra counters: "What a laugh! Can't they give me credit for one tiny thing?"

'Stealing People's Mail' owed much to Biafra's abiding affection for '60s garage rock. "That was the first rock 'n' roll I ever heard. Even later, when I was blundering

Right: Page from *Fallout* #4, March 1981, featuring a collage designed by Jayed Scotti.

Meet the masters of **WORLD WAR III**

It began with a twisted dream... MADE IN U.S.A.

into Music Machine, 13th Floor Elevators and Seeds albums for next to nothing in second-hand shops, I realised how much I still liked that music. And how those songs were written and put together in a different way from Led Zeppelin songs. Another inspiration for 'Stealing People's Mail' was the Screamers, too. That was kind of the structure of it; it could be played on a distorted keyboard as well. We even brought Paul Roessler from the Screamers up to play on the studio version of that song, and he wound up doing the solo instead of Ray, who played something completely different live." Roessler would also provide keyboard accompaniment to 'Drug Me' alongside Ninotchka.

In terms of pushing the envelope, the frantic 'Drug Me' predicted the light-speed thrash Dead Kennedys would explore through *In God We Trust, Inc.* – which in turn became a staging post for the coming 'hardcore' generation. 'Drug Me' seemed almost a manifesto statement, as if they were pushing themselves musically as far as they possibly could. "I don't know what we were thinking!" admits Ray. "Nowadays, with ProTools, we could make everything lock up perfectly. But we were just playing it. Now that you mention it, 'let's see how fast we can play this and make it still hang together but still rock out?' I guess there was a little bit of that." It became something of a rod for their own backs, however. "It was impossible to play that song live," notes Klaus. "I've got videos of us doing it live. We did it, amazingly enough, but I'm sure that was the one we had to record most times in the studio to get it right . . . sure, we were trying to push as hard as we could. 'Stealing People's Mail' was rippingly fast as well, whereas 'Let's Lynch the Landlord' is pretty straight ahead. If anyone wants to do their study, they can find the roots of *that* riff real easy." We're thinking the Blues Magoos' old Nuggets classic, '(We Ain't Got) Nothing Yet'.

The lyric to 'Drug Me' bounces between the fantastical and the utterly mundane – from 'fuck machines' to 'crossword puzzles'. "Part of what I was getting at was not just chemical additions," Biafra says, "but what David Thomas of Pere Ubu called 'Psychobulk' in his interview with *Search And Destroy*. That's where you have television, or some other thing to go in and out of your head, but not be remembered, as kind of a soothing narcotic. That's the crossword puzzles. And thus trends, and fads and rock 'n' roll. I didn't put TV in the lyric, because that's such an obvious example."

Its sheer velocity, the evolution was conceptual as well as musical. "Sometimes I have this problem," notes Biafra, "where I visualise – or hear a song or a riff in my head – and usually it will be a lot slower than how I think it ought to sound with an actual band. So that one didn't just seem to click when it was slower, and it was supposed to be one of those manic, Screamers-type songs. Even if I started out trying to do one type of song, it would often come out sounding completely different. I might think Screamers on the verse, and then something completely different on the chorus. I might think Screamers-*vibe* on the verse, cos it's not like I was taking their riffs or anything."

'Viva Las Vegas', meanwhile, was a perfect choice for album closer. "'Viva Last Vegas' began a Dead Kennedys' tradition that I've carried on to this day of picking very unlikely cover tunes," continues Biafra, "something that will send a shock wave through the crowd – 'what the hell are they playing *that* for?' We never covered 'I Wanna Be Your Dog' or 'Folsom Prison Blues' [though Biafra did record backing vocals to the Red Rockers' studio version]. And we didn't follow all the '70s bar bands and cover Chuck Berry's songs – to the point where it would ruin Chuck Berry for life for a lot of people. It was Ted who suggested covering 'Viva Las Vegas'. Being mostly unfamiliar with Elvis at the time, I'd never heard the song and I'd never even heard of the movie. And once I heard it I thought, yeah, that would be pretty funny. Let's do it."

Biafra revelled in the role of hyperventilating punk crooner, as if to the manner born. "It wasn't the way I did it live. When I tried it that way in the studio, it was so funny I kept it. I also tried 'Kill The Poor' in a Bryan Ferry voice as a gag, but we ended up not using it. Back then I really had trouble hitting the high note at the beginning, then I thought – I should try [Undertones vocalist] Feargal Sharkey! Then I hit it. But we learned songs slowly. They usually took a while to gel. It meant that we didn't learn a lot of other covers, just for the sake of being able to rotate them in the set. We tried that early on by adding The Who's 'Boris The Spider', but our version wasn't particularly interesting. Carlos said afterwards that he thought it was pointless trying to keep up with a new song for every single show, even if it was a cover, and not coming up with *good* songs. And he had a point."

The whole album sounded unlike anything that had preceded it. There were enough elements that were demonstrably 'punk' to locate it within that genre, but otherwise it looked, sounded and felt *different*. "I would say this is probably the responsibility, or mostly had to do with Biafra," suggests Ted, "not compromising the music, and not turning into a reggae band, or having that more Clash-type pop influence, but sticking to his guns. It's one thing I respect about the guy – this is the band, and this is the sound, and we're not going to be something we're not just to be more commercial."

"The thing about *Fresh Fruit*," notes Ray, "is that it had the variety of songs. There were the hardcore songs like 'Drug Me', the neo-psychedelic songs like 'Holiday In

Cambodia', the more art songs like 'Ill In The Head' and pop songs like 'Kill The Poor'. We all liked different types of music. All music doesn't have to be political. And all punk music doesn't have to be political. And it doesn't have to be serious. That's one of the joys of Dead Kennedys. There's a lot of tongue-in-cheek stuff. We really weren't advocating killing the poor – that was satire." Klaus concurs. "There was serious stuff going on where we used humour. It goes back to the Lenny Bruce thing. You use humour to point out the disaster that's going on around you, otherwise you can't take it. We were inspired by people like The Residents and Devo, and Zappa, for taking music and making it make fart noises, basically."

Aside from 6025's 'Forward To Death' and Ray's 'Your Emotions', the lyrics were overwhelmingly Biafra's. "One of the influences I had on Biafra and his lyrics was to try to make them more timeless," says Ray, in one of his more implausible claims. "I suggested some lyric changes, because my thing is, you've got to change it from journalism to poetry. Like at the beginning of 'I Kill Children', the original lyrics are: 'The Ayatollah told me to skin you alive'. I suggested he change it to 'God told me to skin you alive'. Cos how many people remember Ayatollah Khomeni?" Biafra snarls at the suggestion. "Change my lyrics? They never once did anything of the kind. They never read them, much to my heartbreak. The Khomeni reference was *not* the original. The original was always 'God told me to skin you alive'. I got it out of one of those little religious comic books by Chick Publications [the corny über-right wing religious publisher whose output also inspired Alice Donut's disturbing 'Lisa's Father']. That's where I got it from."[11]

Iain McNay flew out to California to meet the band and hear the album. "I hadn't spoken [to the band] directly, but it was arranged through a guy called Craig Hammond, whom I'd met in London. Craig was a part-time DJ, with a huge record collection. He provided a small service where he would get your records out to good radio stations and DJs in America who would play our sort of records. He knew the band, so he was kind of a contact person. When I went over, he picked me up from the airport and drove around to the flat where I met them. They had pretty much the finished album. It wasn't mixed, but it was all recorded. I asked to hear it. They were having a bit of a party at the time. I remember sitting in the kitchen on my own with the kitchen door closed, listening to it on a cheap portable tape recorder; that was the only thing I could listen to it on. In a way, that was quite a good thing. It's always much better to hear something on the medium that most people will hear it rather than a super expensive system in the studio. They were making a noise in the next room, and I was straining to hear this album I'd spent $10,000 on to see what it was like. I immediately liked the album. I spent a bit of time with the band, and with Biafra. I went back to London and the master tapes from the album followed fairly shortly afterwards, and the artwork and everything else."

Said artwork, Biafra's concept, featured a Judith Calson still from the *San Francisco Examiner*, picturing a row of burning police cars. It was taken in 1979 in the wake of the White Night Riots after a verdict of voluntary manslaughter was returned against former police officer Dan White, who had shot gay rights campaigner Harvey Milk and Mayor George Moscone and escaped with a three-to-five-year sentence. White's lawyers claimed he had eaten too many 'Twinkie' cakes on the day before the killing and the consequent sugar rush unbalanced him. The 'Twinkie Defence', a term coined by satirist Paul Krassner, has since become acknowledged shorthand for a spurious or improbable legal defence. Biafra would return to the subject in the rewritten lyrics to the band's cover of 'I Fought The Law' (amending the lyric to 'I fought the law and I won' and finally 'I *am* the law, so I won'). Another of his mayoral policy strands was for the installation of concessions in public spaces to allow citizens to throw rotten fruit at specially erected statues of White, "perhaps the most hated man in San Franciscan history," according to the *San Francisco Weekly*.

However, the sleeve reproduction lost some of the clarity of the image; the grainy monochrome finish meaning that, to this uninitiated purchaser at least, it resembled a traffic jam wreathed in its own smog rather than a riot scene. When the record was released domestically by IRS, they thoughtfully added an orange tint to the flames to distinguish them. "It wasn't just the flames," notes Biafra, "it was the whole photo! Orange and white with black DK lettering. Totally ruined it!" Biafra insisted they change it back and denounced it thus at a 1981 show at Washington's 9:30 Club: "Some of you stooped so low as to buy our wonderful album, even with the shitty Disneyland orange cover which was not our idea."

The rear cover artwork proved even more problematic. After release, the album was subject to a lawsuit from the Sounds Of Sunshine, who had enjoyed a minor hit with a cheesy version of 'Love Means Never Having To Say You're Sorry'. They'd been pictured in wholesome fashion in a 1971 photo (although the uninitiated would have supposed it to be much older than that). They didn't take kindly to either the DKs symbol or the skull and crossbones superimposed on their instruments. "The back cover came from a glossy photo that Klaus used to have nailed to his bedroom door that he had found at a garage sale," Biafra explains. "There was no photographer or band credit on it anywhere. It came to their attention when a sports writer, of all people, reviewed *Fresh Fruit* in a suburban LA daily newspaper, and the paper ran the photo saying it was us! Then they came out of the woodwork and sued us. It turned out most of the people involved in the band were now hardcore, right-wing Christians. The song they particularly objected to was 'I Kill Children', especially the first few lines, which they quoted in their press release. Ever since then, from crazy preachers on TV to Tipper Gore's anti-music crusade, it's those lines of 'I Kill Children' that are quoted in order to condemn Dead Kennedys. I don't think anyone from Tipper Gore on down knew what the rest of the song lyrics were. In other words, the religious right backlash started with the people on the back of the album cover. The woman, in particular, objected to that photo because she didn't want her current gospel music fans to know she had ever had a beehive hairdo. Ironically, IRS Records paid out a settlement to them, possibly more than they ever paid the band." Subsequent copies saw Cherry Red remove the heads of each figure, though this decorative decapitation was done without authorisation from the band.[12]

The album came with a lavish collage poster of bizarre press cuttings collated and curated over several years by Biafra. "I did it in thirty-six hours straight. Among other things, I was listening to Joy Division's *Closer* album for the first and only time, after I'd got it earlier that day. I was listening to it as the sun came up and I realised how late it was. The poster still wasn't done. McNay's deadline was fast approaching and the clock was ticking. A lot of the images I'd had up on my bedroom wall as a teenager in Colorado for years, and people used to like to come over and look at it. And without putting it into words, just criss-crossing all those surreal images in their minds made people think. I wanted to do some special art after seeing the foldout artwork that Crass was coming up with. I thought, wow, imagine if Crass was funny! All I have to do is condense my bedroom walls into a collage poster, and there it will be. No explanation, but you'll look at it again and again. Winston Smith came by the house, after the first thirty hours, and added a few things himself. But most of it was me. I couldn't find any poster paper. So I got promo posters from stores. That's the reason that Travolta and Olivia Newton John from the *Grease* cover are defaced on one side of the poster. All I had to paste the pictures on was a promo poster for the *Grease* soundtrack album!"

Winston Smith, a self-confessed 'graphic wise-cracker', had been introduced to Biafra through a mutual friend who helped with the artwork on a magazine produced by the San Francisco chapter of Rock Against Racism. Biafra already knew of his work – in particular a three-dimensional image of a cross, constructed out of dollar bills, entitled 'Idol'. It would later be used as the artwork for Dead Kennedys' mini-LP *In God We Trust, Inc.* Smith sent over a postcard with a still of JFK's brain exploding taken from the Abraham Zapruder film sequence. On the back of subsequent correspondence, which included exchanging samples of Smith's collage work and fake 'Masterscam' credit cards, they would become firm friends. Or perhaps partners in crime.

Smith remembers spending "several nights well into the wee hours working together on the double-sided composition that became the album's central insert feature. That was truly a labour of love. Not quite sure where the original is anymore. Probably stashed in Biafra's closet – next to the 'jar with Hitler's brain in it'!" Smith was also responsible for the DKs logo, subsequently among the most reproduced and recognisable insignia of the world-wide punk movement, on the label and rear sleeve.

One crucial near derailment was still to be averted, however, as Biafra recollects. "Iain was so desperate to get the album out ahead of all the other full releases (a smart move – more press coverage) he skipped so much as sending us a test pressing. Then the album came out and we discovered to our horror that not only had the mastering engineer Kevin Metcalfe calibrated his machine wrong so all the bass and bottom end was gone, but he had run the tape too fast! Talk about careless. This means that those who bought the album first [and presumably those reviewing it] were rewarded with a cartoon *Fresh Fruit* on helium! One of the first things we did when we got to England was to properly remaster the album with another engineer straight away, along with the 'Kill The Poor'/'In-Sight' single. The lack of care on this was another contributing factor to our departure from Cherry Red."

The critical reaction to the album was underwhelming. John Tobler at *Zig Zag* was a fan, but UK 'inkies' proved more prickly. Andy Gill at *NME*, while admiring *Fresh Fruit*'s "grasp of dynamics" and "highly ordered arrangements", ultimately dismissed it for hitting targets well wide of the mark – "if indeed, the arrows are anything more than little barbs of punky vaudeville". In America, both Robert Christgau and Lester Bangs were equally sniffy, the former being particularly withering, especially about Biafra's "Tiny Tim vibrato".

Overleaf: Pages from Dead Kennedys 'Hard Rock' comic, originally published by Revolutionary Comics. Words by Deena Dasein, artwork by Joe Paradise, stuff by Jay Allen Sanford.

JELLO ALLOWS THE CROWD TO SHRED HIS CLOTHING.

KEEP YOUR PANTS ON!

AT THE PIT IN SAN FRANCISCO, THE DANCE CALLED "THE BIAFRA" IS INVENTED. THE CLUB OD'S THAT SAME NIGHT.

IN BERKELEY, AT AITOS...

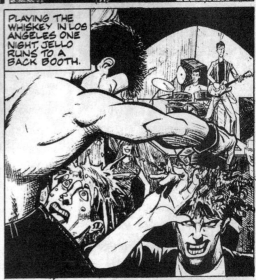

PLAYING THE WHISKEY IN LOS ANGELES ONE NIGHT, JELLO RUNS TO A BACK BOOTH.

RETURNING TO THE STAGE...

WHY'D YOU DO THAT?!

SHOCK IS A WAY OF UNGLUING THE INSIDES OF PEOPLES' HEADS!

THAT GUY YOU SHAMPOOED WITH BEER AND BUTTS WAS FROM RCA RECORDS!

HE WAS CHECKING US OUT!

9

Fresh fruit for Rotting Vegetables

EAST BAY RAY - Guitar   KLAUS FLOURIDE - Bass and Vocals   TED - Drums   JELLO BIAFRA - Vocals

1
KILL THE POOR
(Biafra, Ray)
FORWARD TO DEATH
(6025)
WHEN YA GET DRAFTED
(Biafra)
LET'S LYNCH THE LANDLORD
(Biafra)
DRUG ME
(Biafra)
YOUR EMOTIONS
(Ray)
CHEMICAL WARFARE
(Biafra)

2
CALIFORNIA ÜBER ALLES
(Biafra, Greenway)
I KILL CHILDREN
(Biafra)
STEALING PEOPLES' MAIL
(Biafra)
FUNLAND at the BEACH
(Biafra)
ILL IN THE HEAD
(6025, Biafra)
HOLIDAY IN CAMBODIA
(Dead Kennedys)
VIVA LAS VEGAS
(Pomus and Schuman)

Produced by Norm
Engineered by Oliver Dicieco

Production Assistance - R. Pepperell
Recorded at Mobius Music
Mastered by Kevin Metcalfe
Executive Babysitter - Craig Hammond
Additional Musicians:
Paul Roessler - Keyboards on Drug Me and Stealing Peoples'
Mail
6025 - Other guitar on Ill in the Head
Ninotchka - Keyboard on Drug Me
Special Thanks to the ROCKY MOUNTAIN ARSENAL
CHOIR (Dirk Dirkson, Bobby Unrest, Michael Snyder, Bruce
Calderwood, Geoffrey Lyall, Eric Boucher, Ninotchka,
Barbara Hellbent, HyJean, Curt and ChiChi) for the Clubhouse
Scene in Chemical Warfare

Sleeve Concept - Biafra
Artwork - Annie Horwood
Front Cover photograph by J. Calson, reproduced courtesy
of the San Francisco Examiner
DK logo by Fallout Productions

P & C 1980 Cherry Red Records
199 Kingston Road,
London SW 19
Distributed by Spartan
London Road,
Wembley,
Middlesex,
Exported by Caroline Exports,
56 Standard Road,
London NW 10

To find Dead Kennedys please write:
c/o ALTERNATIVE TENTACLES DIVINE LIGHT MISSION
Post Office Box 5528
San Francisco 94101
California U.S.A.

Also available:
Cherry 13 - 'Holiday in Cambodia /Police Truck' 45
F12 - 'California Über Alles/The Man with the Dogs' 45 on Fast
Products

Manufactured in England by
VINEYARD PRODUCTIONS
56 Standard Road
London NW10

CHERRY RED RECORDS LTD

124

DEAD KENNEDYS

DEAD KENNEDYS
FRESH FRUIT FOR ROTTING VEGETABLES

P&C 1980
CHERRY
RED RECORDS
B RED 10

FACE UP
1 KILL THE POOR
2 FORWARD TO DEATH
3 WHEN YA GET DRAFTED
4 LET'S LYNCH THE
   LANDLORD
5 DRUG ME
6 YOUR EMOTIONS
7 CHEMICAL WARFARE

FACE DOWN
1 CALIFORNIA UBER
   ALLES ◆
2 I KILL CHILDREN
3 STEALING PEOPLES'
   MAIL
4 FUN LAND at the BEACH
5 ILL IN THE HEAD
6 HOLIDAY IN CAMBODIA
7 VIVA LAS VEGAS ◆

STEREO
33⅓RPM

Produced by Norm
Engineered by Oliver Dicicco
℗1980 Virgin Music (Publishers) Ltd.
except ◆©Sound Diagrams and ● ©
Carlin Music Corp.
Manufactured by Vineyard
Productions

Previous pages: *Fresh Fruit For Rotting Vegetables* – UK first pressing and edited rear cover photograph from second pressing following lawsuit 1980 (Cherry Red)

Above: *Fresh Fruit For Rotting Vegetables* labels – Australian, Brazilian, US, Polish, German and Greek 1980-81

Previous pages: *Let Them Eat Jellybeans* compilation album 1981 (Alternative Tentacles)

the FINAL CONFLICT
Now Showing in a Country Near You

Chapter 7

Don't Forget to Pack a Wife

The first condition of understanding a foreign country is to smell it.
(Rudyard Kipling)

ead Kennedys would build on their reputation in Europe with three tours in two years, the first supported by UK Decay, which proved an eye-opener for all involved. Biafra would do "almost anything to get a reaction," recalls Bill Gilliam. He notably introduced to the UK the art of stage-diving as a participatory sport. "One of the reasons to jump into crowds is because then you're no longer a performer talking down at the audience," Biafra states. "You're one and the same." It may be a dubious legacy but it started out well intentioned. As Gilliam remembers: "No-one had ever done that in this country. It was really the start of something. Kids loved it, the stage-diving. The first tour, one of the main problems was restraining the security. At every gig they'd see the audience going crazy, thought that the place was going to get smashed up, and it was a job to keep them calm." The band was generally impressed by the intelligence of the audiences and, bouncers aside, relished the lack of testosterone-fuelled violence that was creeping into the American punk scene.

On the back of the album Dead Kennedys started their mini-tour with a show at the Taboo in Scarborough on 25 September 1980 after a proposed gig at Middlesborough Rock Garden was switched. The hero worship got a little out of hand, with Klaus having his glasses stolen as a trinket. They were returned at the door, as the Klepto-Klaus fan made his exit. Steve Harland was one of the Boro' boys who made the trip. "My memories of the gig are – they were so loud, probably the loudest band, bar Slade, I had ever witnessed live. As they went off some wag in the crowd stole Klaus's glasses – so a request went out if we wanted the DKs to do an encore the bass player wanted his glasses back first – or they wouldn't be coming back on! We had to wait fifteen minutes before his glasses were returned and the DKs came back, but by then the impetus from the gig had evaporated." Rich Teale was also in the audience. "The place was jam-packed with the crowd going mad. The bouncers at Taboo were well known for being heavy-handed and quite a few people were thrown out although there was no violence. It was at the end of the set that someone nicked Klaus's glasses, so the band refused to do an encore until he got them back, which he did, so there was a delay of a few minutes. 'Too Drunk To Fuck' was played and was introduced as a new song. The band had nowhere to stay that night and stopped at Gary Bennett's, a mate of mine's."

A subsequent date in Dundee was cancelled by the local council on the premise that their presence might alienate residents of Alexandria, the American city they were twinned with. As a result, all four members of Dead Kennedys were 'banned for life'. It wasn't just city elders who found the band's presence on our shores irksome, however. *Sounds* critic Dave McCullough paid them the following back-handed compliment. "Dead Kennedys coming to Europe and England is the silliest, most wretchedly useless conceit I've heard all year. Why aren't they pushing *Fresh Fruit* in America where it's urgently needed instead of peddling it second-hand in England?"

Ray recalls the sniffy critical reception in the UK. "The Sex Pistols and The Clash were English, and I think there was at that time the tendency in Europe to think you had all the good bands and there wasn't much coming out of America. In America, punk rock was not part of the mainstream record business. It was really independent, and it made it even harder to get stuff, while The Clash and Sex Pistols were on major labels and got world-wide distribution."

Further dates, including one on 8 October at the Lyceum, were also pulled, with a switch to London's Music Machine instead. The cancellations were intractably linked to the band's name, Biafra telling the *NME* that: ". . . it's designed, not only to torpedo an annoying form of religion that's sprung up around the Kennedys, but also to get under people's skin and annoy them and thereby opening ways of using it as bait. Once they've found out that far, then they're gonna find out about more things that we want them to know about that they don't wanna hear about but should."

Mick McGee saw it all first-hand. "I was seventeen in 1980 making me fourteen in '76, living in the north with my own band Mayhem. We were having our own thing in Liverpool, Manchester, Leeds and Sheffield. To me, *Fresh Fruit* was an injection of new blood; bands, lyrics, outlooks from America in the 'punk's not dead but dying' era of the next wave of '80s punk. I heard 'Über Alles' and was mesmerised totally, off the scale at its time. The tour was announced after the release of 'Cambodia'. By now these clandestine bastards were pounding out of every orifice of punk venues in England."

McGee made every DKs gig on that first tour, and every subsequent show too. "The first date was the Taboo in Scarborough – I had no cash so decided to hitch. Keeping in mind the Yorkshire Ripper was on the loose and terrorising a vast area that the tour was passing through, getting a lift wasn't easy and we found the more stupidly we behaved – handstand cartwheels notwithstanding – the better the chance of a lift. We arrived at Scarborough via an open-top silage truck. The venue looked from the outside like a tattoo shop – pink day-glo frontage in a side street. This was the first and last time I put a dollar in the DKs' pocket. We ended up upstairs playing the pinball machines. An American guy was hanging around and we got talking and sussed he was connected to the band. He gave me a pass to the next gig in Edinburgh. At this time Brit punks were into the leather studs and bristles look – the DKs were not. This was the first time most of the audience had seen Jello and the boys and it was not what they'd expected. They generally looked like some guys off the street and could well have been the potential victims of said leather-clad mad dogs. All these preconceptions went out the window with the opening chord. It was blistering. The guy who had given me the pass was now bare-chested and utterly consumed in fronting his band. Klaus was almost dwarfed by the massive green bass strapped round his neck emblazoned with the 'Danish' DK bumper sticker. Ray looked almost Goth-like, pale-skinned and jet black hair. Ted was mister average nailing his kit. Edinburgh was a long way to hitch but I was going. The gig was at a venue with two performance spaces and Gary Numan was playing. This was a recipe for destruction with two long queues of hardcore punks and electro heads meeting head on at the door. Great gig and off to Liverpool. By this time I had realised that the whole tour shot up and down England and I don't mean progressively working up then down – it literally went north then south then north again. My thumb was getting RSI at some point."

The Liverpool Brady's show (formerly Eric's) on 29 September took place after the defeat of Alan Minter by Marvin Hagler in a middleweight championship bout at Wembley two days previously – which ended in a riot with racist overtones. In a show of sympathy, the audience sieg-heiled the visiting 'imperialist' American punks. Knowing the Eric's crowd, you would think they were more than likely taking the piss. McGee concurs. "Brady's was in the basement of an old city warehouse across the road from the original Cavern," he notes, "It was a punk bastion frequented by all types of hardcore believers, one of whom was a guy called Gary, or 'Gary Fast-Dance' as we named him. Gary had one individual style of dance and it *wasn't* fast. In fact, he swayed slowly in his ankle-length Mac at exactly the same speed to every thrash track that was played and 'Über Alles' was a favourite. Gary incorporated a Nazi salute at the chorus with no other intention than to emphasise the irony of the lyrics and this caught on. Soon the whole club was mimicking it."

"I got to the gig early," McGee continues, "and chatted to Grizzly who worked for the PA crew, Scan. The crew had by now seen me hanging around before the gigs and I gave them a hand getting the gear in and out. Grizz wasn't too happy as someone had thrown up all over the mixing desk the night before and they had spent a good part of the night cleaning it. He wasn't in the mood for any grief from the 'boisterous' Liverpool lads queuing outside. Brady's was small and bloody hot. UK Decay warmed up the crowd and did well despite the drummer having somehow broken his hand and being in plaster on stage. When the Kennedys came on the place took off; they had been waiting a long time for this gig and John Peel had been raving about and playing tracks from *Rotting Vegetables*. As usual the crowd were taking the piss in between songs. All good stuff. I know, I played Eric's/Brady's many times with my band Mayhem and knew that if you couldn't deal with Scouse wit, or if they could find any chink in your armour and you went on the back foot, they would rip the living shit out of you. Klaus' bass rumbled into 'California' backed by Ted's toms, pounding out that familiar beat. The crowed erupted. Then it was like an accident about to happen that you can't stop – as the DKs reached the chorus the whole crowd in complete unison gave the Nazi salute. As far as the eye could see there were outstretched arms. The Kennedy express jumped the tracks and a momentary silence followed. 'What are you doing? That's not what this is about, we ain't Nazis!' bellowed Biafra. He went on to berate the crowd for a good five minutes. I felt I should have told Biafra that they were far from racist – Liverpool is fully aware of its history in the slave trade and had a good multicultural mix. It wasn't meant with any malice but a comment later about a boxer left Liverpool and Biafra with a bad taste in their mouths. I spoke to Biafra after the show and I said I would give him the heads up on anything I thought he should know about the rest of the gigs. My contact with the band had been limited to pre and post gig 'hi' and 'byes' but now I was of some use to them."

Tickets for the show at the Leadmill in Sheffield on 3 October were doctored to 'Ded Kennedys' as a compromise with the city council. It turned out to be quite an evening. "Crazy," notes *Our Generation* author Tony Beesley, "Jello threatened to bang out any more gobbing punks and they stopped, but the beer was still getting thrown constantly. Jello dived into the audience and it was mental – the place appeared to be falling down at the time, there was no roof in places."

One of the people who *didn't* see the DKs at the Sheffield Leadmill was Damon Fairclough. "Flailing; venomous; they came screaming by: and in those brief moments of noise and dread, the Dead Kennedys were ciphers for things that I never suspected. A president had his head demolished in order that they should be so named; the West Coast scene from which they sprang was fired by a muscle-bound political viciousness that was focused and motivated; the language they used wasn't subtly ironic – it was sarcasm wielded as brutally as a nightstick. 'I Kill Children' indeed. These things were all but lost on me, but to my dad – always interested in the music I professed to like, and intrigued by punk as a social phenomenon, or as a new folk music – here was cause for alarm. This was not like The Damned, who were feathered and boa-ed with the spirit of the music hall, and who were just a mouthful of gob away from being suitable guests on *The Good Old Days* ... And despite 'You dirty fucker' and the rest of that Bill Grundy pantomime, even the Sex Pistols turned out to be more art school prank than sedition made flesh. Nothing wrong with art school pranks of course, but they don't chill the parental blood quite like the DKs hollering 'This world brings me dowwwwwn, I'm looking forward to death.' When I played the Dead Kennedys, I heard a sound that was scabrous and incandescent, that scorched the teak-effect music centre from whence it came . . . So when I brought home the Dead Kennedys album *Fresh Fruit For Rotting Vegetables* there was much furrowing of brows and hovering in doorways. There was earnest stroking of chins. There were sudden and serious conversations that seemed to come out of nowhere – about songs that said one thing and meant something else, about discussion and argument, about nihilism and protest, about Jello Biafra's visions of AmeriKKKa. I believe there were whispered discussions when I'd gone to bed, undertakings to 'keep an eye on this', and to be watchful, wary of some threat left unspecified but that could tip me into future oblivion. In the autumn of 1980, a school friend of mine returned from the summer break somewhat translated. His hair was cropped spikily short; his natural blond locks were streaked vivid orange . . . this fresh-faced junior punk would bring back reports from his family home, though to us, they may as well have been coming from another universe: his parents owned *Never Mind The Bollocks*; his sister had dyed her pubes green; and then came the news that, aged thirteen, he was going to a gig at the Sheffield Leadmill; he was going to see the Dead Kennedys. HE WAS GOING WITH HIS FUCKING MUM AND DAD! They weren't there to chaperone him, or monitor his activities, or warn him of the dangerous paths that might lie ahead. No. They were there to see the band. That's all. To see the band and spend some time with their son . . . Which went to prove little, except that, in the words of teenagers everywhere: life was so unfair."

Overleaf: Dead Kennedys UK Tour: Liverpool Brady's, 29 September 1980. (Photography by Mick McGee)

Mick McGee continued to hitchhike the rest of the tour. "The PA crew took me under their wings and I did the get ins and outs but was still hitching and sleeping rough and it was heading into winter. I was now working with Scan as a free box pusher; heavy work. Scan took pity on me and allowed me to sleep in the cab of the hire truck. Sadly this did not last long due to my smelly feet so I slept in the back with the gear. The truck became the only thing I was interested in while travelling; it was a joy and reassuring to search the cities and towns and spot the day-glo pink and yellow paint job Edwin Shirley still use today. It meant I had made it to the gig."

"If Biafra was in the mood," McGee continues, "he would soak himself and the audience with water, lots of it from pint glasses. It was everywhere including all over our sleeping bags. On realising this mid-gig I dragged the sodden rags back to the dressing room and draped them over the radiators trying not to soak a grand piano that was in there for some unknown reason. Some time later I headed back to the sweltering dressing room. The door was open and I encountered the most bizarre sound of 'Cambodia' being played on the piano, which was set up there. I also noted the smell – to quote the man, 'it smells like Dakar!' On entering I saw it was Ted playing the piano who on seeing me launched with the rest of the band into a rousing chorus of 'Right Guard will not help you here!' They were fucking right – it stank!"

The final gig was at, of all places, West Runton Pavilion in Cromer. "The bouncers were a local rugby team-cum-wannabe bikers," recalls McGee. "I recall one of them saying he 'couldn't wait to get his hands on one of the spiky fuckers' as he set up a scoreboard for him and his mates to see how many punks they could squish. At 11am it looked like a quiet rural village but by 6.30pm it was madness. Coachload after coachload of stoned, drunk punks shipped in from neighbouring towns and fell out of the doors. One of the drivers collapsed from passive glue inhalation. The bouncers got out of control and me and Micro overruled them but not before 'dick-for-brains' claimed his first point – a vomiting young kid who could hardly stand up." Meanwhile, Biafra introduced the as then largely unheard 'Too Drunk To Fuck' thus. "One of these days this song will come out as a single – if we're allowed to make any more records. It's our universal pop song we figure everyone can relate to . . ."

The remixed 'Kill The Poor' was concurrently released as the third single from the album. McNay devised a promotional campaign using a photograph of the Conservative Party conference with the party banner airbrushed out to read 'Kill The Poor' instead. "I thought, if the magazines and newspapers see the advert in advance," McNay recalls, "they won't let me run it. So I found out what their dead-lines were and delivered it a few minutes before, so it would be hard to pull it. We got it in all the magazines and weeklies. We did get taken to an advertising complaints tribunal. But all they said was, don't run that advert again, which of course we had no intention of doing."

Originally, McNay had been keen to see 'Viva Las Vegas' released as the third single. "I thought we could get daytime Radio One on that. Obviously Peel had played 'Cambodia', and I think Mike Read played 'Cambodia' as well. I thought it wouldn't be too difficult to extend it. We wouldn't have got *The Breakfast Show*, but we would have got late afternoon shows for 'Viva Las Vegas'. I was very keen on this and even scheduled it. Then Biafra said no, he didn't want to release it. I said fair enough, but we'd got partly down the line on that, and even organised a plugger to work on it. I thought we could have had a Top 40 hit with that track and broken the band to a whole different audience, but it wasn't to be." McNay would get his hit in 1981 when the band's 'Too Drunk To Fuck' (a song that always owed *something* to The Alley Cats' 'Nothing Means Nothing Anymore') became the first record with the titular expletive to break the Top 40.

Biafra wasn't at all keen on either the release of 'Kill The Poor' or 'Viva Las Vegas'. "'Kill The Poor' was just yanked off the album and a different mix thrown on the single," Biafra affirms, "to derail Iain McNay's scheme to release 'Viva Las Vegas' as a novelty single, confine us to that and move on to another project. We said no, it's going to be 'Kill The Poor', and you're not putting 'In-Sight' out as a flexidisc. We're yanking 'Viva Last Vegas' and putting it on as the b-side, whether you like it or not." Ray claims it was a group decision. "This happened a lot. The band would discuss something, and then Biafra would call Iain and say we don't want to do it. Then Iain assumes Biafra's doing it."

According to Ray, the same thing happened with the media. "Biafra was the front-man and spokesman. And he loved doing interviews. And people presumed because he said it, it was his idea. That's a wrong presumption. A lot of the political ideas were mine, in terms of real solutions to problems. In terms of putting things in a nice slogan, Biafra was brilliant at that. I see things as more complex. All of us, we definitely had discussions. But there are plenty of ideas I see in interviews that people don't attribute to Klaus or me that were probably our ideas originally. That's the way journalists work. But once people talk to me, they realise, hey, he does know what the Federal Reserve does."[13] All of which "really pisses me off," states Biafra. "What

Overleaf: Dead Kennedys UK Tour: Liverpool Brady's, 29 September 1980. (Photography by Mick McGee)

a lie. These guys were fucking *allergic* to interviews! They'd run off and party every night and leave me in the dressing room to do all the interviews even though my throat was shot. This became such a sore point with me that it nearly helped break up the band in '84."

The album performed better than anyone could have envisaged. By 1980, around 30,000 copies had been sold in the UK and it went Top 10 in Finland, Spain, Portugal and Australia. It was the first classic American punk album of the post-CBGB's generation (if we are to lay aside the Germs' storied but patchy *GI* from 1979) with Black Flag's *Damaged* still a year away.

Our story closes in December 1980 when Ted announced his departure, ostensibly to further his architectural studies (though he continued in the Wolvarines, with whom he had been playing intermittently, and who additionally briefly featured Klaus in their ranks). He played his final set with Dead Kennedys that month, before being replaced by D.H. Peligro, whom Biafra had spotted playing with SSI at the Deaf Club and was subsequently invited to audition after bumping into Ray at the Mabuhay. Klaus and Ray are on record as saying Ted's departure resulted from a 'me or him' ultimatum issued by Biafra, but the real reasons were prosaic. "We asked him to leave," confirms Biafra. "The reason was musical differences, that old cliché. And the decision was unanimous. The first order of business in 1981 was finding a new drummer and Peligro debuted that February."

The band also cut the cord with Cherry Red following the June 1981 release of 'Too Drunk To Fuck'. They had been angered by the label's penchant for intensive-farming its back catalogue and McNay's reluctance that Cherry Red become too synonymous with either punk or Dead Kennedys. "We were never on truly bad terms," recalls Biafra, "we just left the label because they were overly exploitative of the catalogue (changing the sleeve and redoing a 12-inch of 'Holiday In Cambodia' and 'Too Drunk To Fuck' to resell the same record, etc.). Plus, in a crucial move, they declined to release *Let Them Eat Jellybeans!* because they 'didn't want to be too closely associated with Dead Kennedys'." The latter was a compilation album through which Biafra intended to highlight the frustrated talents of bands denied the chance Dead Kennedys had enjoyed, including Black Flag, Bad Brains, DOA, the Subhumans and, in a dues-paying thank you for giving the DKs a start in the first place, The Offs. Ultimately many of these bands would be well serviced by the revived Alternative Tentacles, which Biafra resurrected after splitting from Cherry Red in the UK and Faulty Products and Statik in the US – neither of whom, advances aside, ever paid the band a penny.

The first chapter of the Dead Kennedys story was complete. At least two further great albums – as well as lawsuits, police busts, censorship charges, literally riotous gigs, *Penis Landscape*, Tipper Gore and the *Oprah Winfrey Show* lay ahead. Some other poor bastard can tackle that, though.

Overleaf: 'Kill The Poor' / 'In-Sight' – UK release 1980 (Cherry Red)
Overleaf: 'Kill The Poor' / 'Viva Las Vegas' – Spanish promo + first pressing 1981 (Edigsa)
Overleaf: 'Kill The Poor' / 'California Über Alles' – German release 1980 (Hafenklang)
Pages 148-149: Spanish promo information sheet 1981 (Edigsa)

DEAD KENNEDYS/ KILL THE POOR (NEW VERSION OF THE SONG FROM THE ALBUM 'FRESH FRUIT FOR ROTTING VEGETABLES' CAT.NO.B RED 10) B/W IN-SIGHT (PREVIOUSLY UNRELEASED TRACK). FRONT COVER DRAWING BY GREG WRIGHT/ DRAWINGS ABOVE © 1980 FALLOUT PRODUCTIONS. PRODUCED BY NORM.

Ⓟ&© 1980 CHERRY RED RECORDS, 199 KINGSTON ROAD, LONDON SW19 DISTRIBUTED BY SPARTAN, LONDON ROAD, WEMBLEY, MIDDLESEX

Imp. POLYGRAM INDUSTRIES MESSAGERIES
Imprimé et fabriqué en France

15S0079   1

DE MAXIMO
INTERES
DEAD KENNEDYS

CARA A:
MATAD A LOS POBRES
(KILL THE POOR), 3'02''
(Biafra, Ray)

CARA B:
VIVA LAS VEGAS, 2'32''
(Pomus and Schuman)

Extraido del L.P. «Fresh fruit for Rotting Vegetables»

Edita. EDIGSA, Gran Via de les Corts Catalanes, 594. Barcelona-10
Imprime. I. G. Coballfo, Cobalto, 172. Hospitalet de Llobregat
Dep. leg. B. 1554-1981

 INFORMACION

Dead Kennedys

Los últimos punk de la ciudad.

Según todos los indicios, que no son pocos, los funerales por el inherte y aún ruidoso cadáver punk ya han sido celebrados. Cronistas e historiadores han embalsamado convenientemente estas cuatro bárbaras letras para dejar un testimonio de su paso por este mundo a futuras generaciones. Una polvorienta lápida se erige en el Cementerio del Rock, y los restos punk yacen, todavía convulsionados, bajo ella.

Sin embargo, y ateniéndose a la más elemental regla del punk que es el inconformismo, una nueva tormenta, con sus pertinentes rayos y truenos, se han desatado para derrumbar sin miramientos todas las cómodas conjeturas del observador. El punk puede estar muerto como leyenda o fenómeno, pero no como realidad. Y desde la lejana y pacífica Costa Oeste estadounidense, vía Londres, cuatro temerarios supervivientes se obstinan en atosigar los, hasta ahora, tranquilizados tocadiscos con nuevos mensajes repletos de blasfemias, electricidad, insultos y adrenalina. Cuatro adiestrados guerrilleros del punk que responden al irrespetuoso nombre de DEAD KENNEDYS (Los Kennedys muertos) y que han concentrado su indomable insistencia de kamizake en el LP "Fresh Fruit For Rotting Vegetables" (Fruta Fresca por Verdura Podrida).

Los antecedentes de DEAD KENNEDYS se remontan a 1978. Año éste en el que un individuo censado como Jello Biafra regresa a San Francisco, su ciudad natal, tras asistir al parto del punk en Londres.Como Frisco resulta ser un reumático bastión del hippismo y otras delicias por el estilo -véase el star system del cercano Hollywood o la cultura del surf asentada a lo largo y ancho de California -el mencionado Biafra decide divulgar las visiones que la Sodoma del Rock, Londres para más señas, le han proporcionado. Encargándose él mismo

148

de cantar, componer y presidir, reune al taquicárdico guitarrista
East Bay Ray -también conocido como Ray Valium- el bajista Klaüs
Flouride y el batería Ted y bautiza a la banda con el significativo
DEAD KENNEDYS.

Ante la hostilidad general, los DEAD KENNEDYS, empiezan a asestar
golpes veniales al confortable armazón que protege las soleadas tar
des californianas. Mientras en la otra costa, Nueva York, son varios
los defensores del punk, en California parece que solo luchan Biafra
y sus Kennedys. El 19 de julio de este mismo año dan su primer con-
cierto y meses más tarde Jello Biafra se presenta a las elecciones
para la alcaldía de San Francisco que como se puede suponer, pierde.
Dado que ningún sello americano se ofrece a canalizar comercialmente
sus arrebatos sonoros, aceptan la propuesta de Fast Records, un pe-
queño sello de Edimburgo, y graban el primer single. " California
über Alles " utiliza los tres minutos de duración para atacar a Jerry Brown, por aquel entonces gobernador de California, y asustar un
poco a los bienpensantes del lugar. Para el 79, cuando se aprecian
los primeros síntomas de extinción en el punk, son fichados por otro
sello británico como Cherry Red Records y graban un nuevo single que
también contiene un poderoso hit para Angeles del Infireno y amantes
del punk-rock a toda velocidad como el perfecto "Holiday in Cambodia". En 1980, siendo ya conocidos por los devoradores de emociones
fuertes, graban "Fresh Fruit For Rotting Vegetables". Un artefacto
espinoso que contiene las dos canciones antes citadas y doce grana-
das más que en este mismo momento están estallando en algún,nuevamen
te, horrorizado tocadiscos. "Kill the Poor", el nuevo single,"Drug
Me", "I Kill the Children" -toda una declaración de pricipios por
parte del grupo- "Funland at the Beach" y un remake del elvispresle
yano "Viva las Vegas" son algunas de ellas.

Catorce cortes de no más de tres minutos de duración, mortíferas mi
niaturas que aceleran la circulación sanguínea en un abrir y cerrar
de ojos,manifestaciones de punk en perfecto estado de salud. Las pro
pias visiones de los DEAD KENNEDYS. Unos profetas en su tierra y los
últimos punks de la ciudad.

                              EDIGSA
                              Departamento de Promoción

149

lividual
into an
ently ig-
erans re-
rom army
sure to

ca seems
r children
t of the
. We are
our autos
Soon they
n children.

OUTSIDE AGITATORS

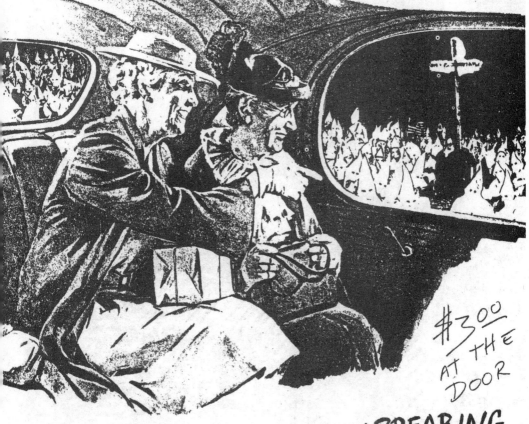

$3.00 AT THE DOOR

PLUS iDioT CHILD APPEARING NOW AT

THE FuKkUPS

& PEER PRESSURE

NICO'S UNDERGROUND
99284 BROADWAY

©FALLOUT 1981

MINORS WELCOME

AMERICA YOU MUST CHOOSE:

THIS OR THIS

AMERICA'S NEW LEADERSHIP

DEAD KENNEDYS

ALTERNATIVE TENTACLES

TOO DRUNK TO FUCK

NEW ON CHERRY RED RECORDS

All You Ever Do Is Complain, Yeah?

I don't like nostalgia. Unless it's mine.

(Lou Reed)

hirty years on, *Fresh Fruit*, the most musically complex punk record ever released as *Mojo* magazine once stated, and arguably the most funny, biting and cerebral, has had colossal influence. Hüsker Dü, Dinosaur Jr., the Pixies, Nirvana, and more recently everyone from Green Day and The Offspring to Massive Attack, The Prodigy and Franz Ferdinand, have absorbed and acknowledged its influence. Biafra, who remains a dyed-in-the-bones fan of the broader punk canon, finds the praise misplaced. "You know enough about this music, as much as I do, that anyone who heard *From the Cradle To The Grave* by the Subhumans, or *Zen Arcade* by Hüsker Dü, or Mission Of Burma, or whatever, would just hotly dispute that." He's pushing at a locked door.

Ted is also stoical when it comes to the warm afterglow of critical adulation for *Fresh Fruit*, and is not convinced that its pioneer status is deserved. "I wouldn't say so, not from my point of view. It was rock 'n' roll. I guess it was different than some other types of punk bands at the time, because there was Ray's surf-sounding guitar, and I didn't play the typical two-four hard-charging punk drumbeats. It was more fluid, I would say. And Klaus's bass was somewhat more melodic than a lot of other bass players at the time. But in terms of it being *avant garde* or reaching new boundaries, I don't know if I really felt that."

He's also the most reserved about its achievements. "To me, it lacks a little depth and punch and is flat-sounding. Some of it has to do with the way it was pressed from the master copy. Some of it also has to do with the way it was actually produced. Some of the albums that I think it could have been closer to, and captured some of the depth, and the punch and the bottom, would be something like the Nirvana album, *Nevermind*. But the overall sound of the album, even today, I think it could be a different album, and have even more of an impact if it was better produced." But

Left: Page from *Fallout* #4, March 1981, by Winston Smith, featuring an advert for the single 'Too Drunk to Fuck'. This was the original cover art, but Biafra later switched it for another image found in a religious tract. Smith later reused the original artwork for a compilation tribute CD of Japanese bands covering Dead Kennedys songs entitled *Get Drunk More Fuck*, released in 2010.

then, Dead Kennedys had $10,000 to work with. Nirvana had somewhat more. And it's also worth pointing out that all three members of the latter band acknowledged the influence of Dead Kennedys at the time and since.

"It set the bar for *us*," says Klaus. "The record sounded different to anything else at the time, which was what we were aiming for. We weren't aiming to sound better, necessarily, just different. To have our own signature sound, and that album established that. We weren't a template for other bands to follow necessarily, as much as a template for ourselves to follow on from that *Fresh Fruit* album. There were a ton of bands that sounded like the Sex Pistols and a ton of bands that sounded like the Ramones. There weren't a whole lot of bands that tried to sound like the Kennedys."

But he enjoys the residual affection among both fans and musicians. "It's hard to take in, sometimes, that people in these bands that I admire already have my stuff. It's a good feeling." Ted agrees: "I'm still amazed. I have kids of my own, and their friends are more interested in the fact that I was in the band than my own children. Any time you hear that, or people my own age, who say, 'Ah, I used to go see you guys,' it's great to hear."

"Fifty years from now," says Ray, "when we've all passed away, the only thing that's really going to matter is the music, and the playing of the record. All the other stuff is a side-show. What's interesting is that *Fresh Fruit* is closer to the start of rock 'n' roll, like the Sun Sessions and Elvis Presley, than it is to today. It's kind of astonishing how much variety there was in the music between 1955 and 1980."

Biafra is in the invidious position of emphasising his belief in what the band achieved while distancing itself from the actions of the reformed group. "To make it clear, I'm very proud of the music, the band, and what we accomplished when we were together. I've tried to maintain that spirit and that set of ethics since that time."

Although it's the best known and most popular album they released, it still isn't Biafra's favourite. "I like *Plastic Surgery Disasters* and *Frankenchrist* more because they're darker, more intricate. They had more musical contributions from other members of the band, believe it or not, and that was one of the reasons. More 'Holiday In Cambodia'-like contributions from other members of the band. It was darker, more unique, more us."

Fresh Fruit did, however, provide him with the sublime satisfaction of getting a roasting from his old adversary, Jared Johnson of the *Denver Post*. "I got a clipping mailed to me," Biafra recalls. "Instead of capsule reviews, Jared Johnson had devoted his entire column to how disgusted he was with *Fresh Fruit For Rotting Vegetables*. I've never felt such a sense of gratification and achievement in my life! That's exactly the impact I wanted it to have."[14]

DEAD KENNEDYS

TOO DRUNK TO

Warning !!

THIS RECORD CONTAINS
LANGUAGE THAT SOME
PEOPLE MAY CONSIDER
SMUTTY, OFFENSIVE,
AND NOT NICE.

DEAD KENNEDYS

CAUTION

YOU ARE THE VICTIM OF YET ANOTHER STODGY RETAILER AFRAID TO WARP YOUR MIND BY REVEALING THE TITLE OF THIS RECORD SO PEEL SLOWLY AND SEE...

Virus 2 1981 I.R.S.,Inc.Printed in USA

A

DEAD KENNEDYS

CHERRY RED RECORDS

45 RPM STEREO

Too Drunk To Fuck

Written by Biafra.
Published by Virgin Music
Publishing Ltd.

CHERRY 24

An Alternative Tentacle Production

℗ © 1981 CHERRY RED
RECORDS LTD

Manufactured in France

Previous pages: 'Too Drunk To Fuck' / 'The Prey' – Australian release 1981 (Missing Link)
Previous pages: 'Too Drunk To Fuck' / 'The Prey' – US release 1981 (Faulty Products)
Previous pages: 'Too Drunk To Fuck' / 'The Prey' Labels – Canadian, Finnish, UK and US releases 1981
Above: 'Too Drunk To Fuck' / 'The Prey' – Irish clear vinyl release 1981 (Cherry Red)
Above right and right: 'Too Drunk To Fuck' / 'The Prey' – UK release 1981 (Cherry Red)
Right: 'Too Drunk To Fuck' / 'The Prey' Label – UK 12" release 1981 (Cherry Red)
Far right: 'Too Drunk To Fuck' / 'The Prey' Label – New Zealand 12" release 1981 (Cherry Red)

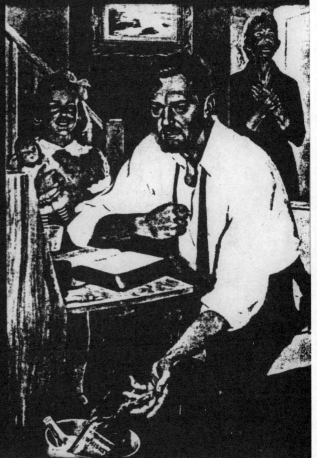

Above: 'Too Drunk To Fuck' / 'The Prey' – Greek release 1981 (Music Box)
Above right: 'Too Drunk To Fuck' / 'The Prey' – Australian 12" release 1981 (Cherry Red)
Right: 'Too Drunk To Fuck' / 'The Prey' – Greek release 1981 (Music Box)
Far right: 'Too Drunk To Fuck' / 'The Prey' – Australian 12" release 1981 (Cherry Red) rear cover

161

Endnotes

1.

It was running 956 for Ray, 1227 for Klaus, 1167 for Biafra and 585 for Ted, trivia fans. Ye gods.

2.

"When I first met him," Biafra states, "Ray had no punk records. He had never heard of The Stooges. So I loaned him a tape and he understood. He probably heard the Ramones etc. on KSAN, an old hippie radio station (especially Howie Klein and Chris Knab's 'Outcast Hour') who actually had punk singles in their regular rotation until the majors told them to stop."

3.

Jello (or Jell-O) was the American trade name for Kraft's nutrition-free gelatine dessert, variously endorsed by comedians Jack Benny and Bill Cosby down the years, and thus a fixture in American consciousness that Europeans might be unaware of. Its alternative uses included employment by female 'mud wrestlers' in strip joints and adult bars. One noted philosopher prior to Mr Boucher also had fun with it; Bertrand Russell had occasion to note that "Rampant Jell-O consumption by the King of England is neither necessary nor sufficient for the existence of God" as a test of propositional logic. The 'surname' Biafra, conversely, was taken from the secessionist state crushed by the Nigerian federal government in the late '60s. After sustained military action, an economic blockade and the destruction of the region's agricultural resources to suppress its participants, close on a million died. "To clarify," Biafra clarifies, "the deaths were largely by mass starvation, covered in gruesome photographic detail in the media. So Biafra, at that time, was the universally recognised symbol of the worst kind of mass genocide. Guess whose delta they found the oil in? Ogoniland overlaps."

4.

An original Healers' take on 'California Über Alles' would be included as a vinyl bonus on the *Rocky Mountain Low* compilation, a lovingly curated round-up of the Colorado scene, issued by Hyperpycnal in 2009. The compilation is also notable for including the two songs by Mark Bliesener (aka Radio Pete), '(Just A) Patsy' and

'Jackie's Song', recorded on 6 July 1976 when he was still in his 'Dead Kennedys head space'.

5.

Another early song, albeit non-rehearsed, that never made vinyl, at least until the idea was revived in 1990 by Biafra in his collaboration with Lard, was 'Sylvestre Matuschka'. It was dedicated to the titular Hungarian mass murderer (real name Szilveszter Matuska) who would masturbate while watching train derailments he had engineered. "I made the mistake of jinxing any earlier versions," Biafra recalls, "by giving out the title in an interview [with *Search And Destroy*] without actually finishing the song first."

6.

Other alternative versions of the song abound. They include covers by The Delgados, Cannibal Corpse side project Six Feet Under, The Deceased and Dramarama. Evidence of its cross-genre and international appeal can best be demonstrated by reference to efforts by Jayne County and the She Wolves, who adapted the lyrics to skewer anti-gay marriage legislation, Italian ska band Iquattrocentocolpi, Belgian industrial/techno pioneer Patrick Stevens of Hypnoskull or Anglo-American fusioneers The Who Boys. The latter performed a 'mash-up' of the song alongside Gil Scott-Heron's 'The Revolution Will Not Be Televised', as 'Revolution Über Alles'. Kennedys' fan and skate legend Tony Hawks included it on his soundtrack for the *American Wasteland* game (predating the inclusion of 'Holiday In Cambodia' on *Guitar Hero III*, which was similarly not without controversy).

Then there's Norwegian metallers Mayhem, who included 'California Über Alles' on their 1987 demo. Though it seems improbable that Øystein Aarseth, aka Euronymous, credited with being the prime mover in the development of black metal before his bass player stabbed him to death, was completely sympathetic to the political dimensions of the song. Further evidence of its international appeal can be found in adaptations by Polish rocker Kazik Staszewski ('Kalifornia Ponad Wszystko') and Hasidic New Wave, who recorded 'Giuliani Über Alles' in protest at the eponymous New York mayor. Disposable Heroes of Hiphoprisy gave the record an industrial hip-hop make-over, though even a lyricist as formidable as Michael Franti struggled to think of a decent rhyme for 'police' other than 'niece' in the middle eight (said relative had now acquired long hair rather than merely being 'uncool').

Franti's take on 'California Über Alles' was included on Virus 100, Alternative Tentacles' centenary release of 1992, which featured sixteen different DKs covers. The artists included Faith No More, the Didjits, Napalm Death, Mojo Nixon, L7, Sepultura, Kramer and Sister Double Happiness, alongside AT affiliates Alice Donut, NoMeansNo, Neurosis and others. Interestingly, and for the sake of any argument that their debut remains the Kennedys' definitive album, of the sixteen songs chosen, eight emanated from *Fresh Fruit*, with a further two (the b-sides 'Police Truck' and 'In-Sight') dating from the period under discussion. Similarly, on the 'reggae/industrial electronica' tribute album *In Dub We Trust*, where Sheep On Drugs tackle 'California', the majority of the material is again drawn from the *Fresh Fruit* era. A third 'tribute' album – *What Were We Fighting For?* – dates from 1998. It features seventeen tracks from a variety of bands you or I have never heard of, Electric Frankenstein and Blanks 77 aside. Anal Cunt are, however, the perfect pairing for *In God We Trust, Inc.*'s 'Religious Vomit' and Politikill Incorrect's infusion of Black Sabbath's 'Paranoid' riff into 'Jock-O-Rama' is worth catching.

And who could forget Duckmandu's 2005 *Fresh Duck for Rotting Accordionists*, a complete re-tread of the whole album on accordion, featuring backing vocals from Klaus as well as a Winston Smith cover. It featured a greatly expanded 'Rocky Mountain Arsenal Memorial Choir of Death', including a returning Dirk Dirksen, as well as Mr. Bungle's Trey Spruance, Greg Ginn of Black Flag, V. Vale and John Gluck of the Punk Rock Orchestra of San Francisco. All good fun, and meritoriously it didn't overdose on ambition by citing itself, humbly, as the 'definitive accordion version' of the album.

"I spent much of my high school years going to Dead Kennedys and other punk shows," recalls Duckmandu, aka Aaron Seeman, "often at the On Broadway [the venue Dick Dirksen also booked directly above the Mabuhay] in San Francisco. Those shows were like religious experiences for me. Slam-dancing (it wasn't called 'moshing' yet) was a kind of group consciousness, where you transcended ordinary physical laws and could accomplish super-physical feats. The level of connectedness, and blurring between, audience and performer at a DK show caused a kind of mass group pulsing of psycho-drama and pseudo-violence which was as deeply cathartic. In part, *Fresh Fruit* was a soundtrack for that experience, but it's also a finely crafted work musically. It has pentatonic blues riffs ('Chemical Warfare', 'Funland At The Beach'), doo-wop chord progressions ('Kill The Poor'), flamenco ('California Über Alles') and more experimental harmonies ('Ill In The Head', 'Forward To Death') all on one album! *Fresh Fruit* is a fucked-up, sped-up, ghost-music-gritty apocalyptic urban reflection of American rock 'n' roll and rock history. That the entire album closes out with a cover of 'Viva Las Vegas' is more than appropriate; Elvis and his version of "Viva Las Vegas" represent the essence of the nightmare the album is commenting on. That Jello managed a parody of Elvis's voice (itself a parody of an Elvis impersonation) while still retaining his unmistakable Jelloness completes the tour de force."

As for the reunited Rocky Mountaineers: "My 'Chemical Warfare' choir was around sixty voices recorded individually and mixed together. As I only had a 16-track recorder, I created three sub-mixes and then mixed them together. The sub-mixes are secret tracks on the CD. I wanted to get some of the original members of the choir from *Fresh Fruit*. I already knew Klaus from the Punk Rock Orchestra, which I helped found. I called SST records to see if they could put me in touch with Greg Ginn and he answered the phone himself! He did his screaming and choking on the spot. Winston Smith and Vick Vale and others I knew or had met around San Francisco. Dirk Dirksen, who I didn't know, was a fun one. I remembered him fondly from his audience-insulting 'Goodbye, get out' speeches at the end of shows at the On Broadway. Once I tracked him down for the choir, I thought it would be fun to record an original 'Goodbye, get out' speech for a last secret track on the CD. He did the screaming and choking with aplomb, but when it came time to record the speech, he said he couldn't work up the anger without actually having the audience of sweaty obnoxious punk rockers in front of him. So I said, 'Look, I *was* one of the sweaty obnoxious punks, so I'll stand here behind your video editor and let me have it.' This led to his personalised attack on me as an accordionist, punk rocker, etc. that you hear on the last track. A fitting ending, and a sad farewell as he died the next year."

'California Über Alles' would later be sampled prominently by The Prodigy on 'Dead Ken Beats'. In performance especially – the chanting of 'Dead Kennedys' not-withstanding – it's quite the show-stopper. They Might Be Giants' John Linnell also played it live. In an ever more unexpected context, there are samples of 'California', as well as elephant roars and police sirens, throughout Tony Matterhorn's bonkers dancehall reggae song 'Big Belly Guns'.

Other *Fresh Fruit* era songs have not been afforded quite the same attention. Attrition's sinister electronic take on 'Kill The Poor' (also covered by death metallers The Agony Scene) is worth a listen, as is the polka version of 'Too Drunk To Fuck' by the Benka Boradovsky Bordello Band. Less so the Finnish ska (I kid you not) effort by The Valkyrians. Dunedin alt-pop legends The Chills had a cut at a rockabilly version of 'Let's Lynch The Landlord' on their 2010 album. The song has also been covered by the Whisky Daredevils, who specialise in giving hardcore punk originals an alt-country twist, as well as Torpedo Monkeys, 13 Bats, Stockholm garage rockers The Nomads and Misterio – founded by Señor Flavio of platinum selling Latin Rock band Los Fabulosos Cadillac. It sounds a bit like The Cramps.

'Holiday In Cambodia' has been covered in styles ranging from cabaret (Richard Cheese), irreverent hillbilly (Red Star Belgrade) and metal (Prisoners Of Earth) as well as contemporary punk (Atreyu). In 2007 the Foo Fighters, alongside Serj Tankian of System Of A Down, ran through it for the benefit of MTV's VMA Fantasy Suites, interestingly enough, incorporating the album version's echoplexed intro and 'Pol Pot' refrain, but substituting 'brothers' for 'niggers' in the lyric. It is doubtful the song has ever been performed to a more inappropriate audience, which is a terrible shame or great idea depending on where you stand on strategic penetration theory. Camp Freddy, the covers band formed by Dave Navarro (Jane's Addiction, Red Hot Chili Peppers), Billy Morrison (Circus Diablo) and Matt Sorum (Guns N' Roses), with Mark McGrath of Sugar Ray on vocals and guest appearances from Lars Ulrich and Robert Trujillo of Metallica, also stuck to the *Fresh Fruit* version. The YouTube clip confirms it to be awful as you might imagine.

There are versions of 'Police Truck' by Thee Exit Wounds, Nailbomb, The Broken Toys, Destructors and LA's original surf punks Agent Orange. Canadian dig-ital hardcore/breakcore project Contra had a stab at 'Your Emotions' – and managed the impressive feat of speeding it up. For an isolated sample of Ray's guitar work on 'Too Drunk To Fuck' you can check Indonesian hip-hop artist Serenada Iblis's 'Too Funk To Hike', or perhaps the Amazing Klingonz pyschobilly take, or that of Japanese band the Kead Dennedys. Nouvelle Vague's now infamous version of 'Too Drunk' amplifies how those songs have survived the transition to different musical idioms. The latter, of course, is the source of yet another fissure between the former band members. Biafra remains livid that it was used in a brutal rape scene in one of Quentin Tarantino's *Grindhouse* movies (actually the *Planet Terror* segment directed by Robert Rodriguez) and approved by his former band-mates.

7.

Washington's Teen Idles (pre-Minor Threat/Fugazi) also made the pilgrimage for a Dead Kennedys show with the Circle Jerks and Flipper at the Mabuhay in August 1980. Though they ended up being kicked off the bill by Dirksen, they noted the all-ages policy at the venue and the 'X' marks on hands indicating those who could not legally be served alcohol. It later became the symbol for the 'straight edge' culture that formulated on their return to Washington. Later both Ian MacKaye and Henry Rollins attended the second 1981 Dead Kennedys Irving Plaza show in New York and sat at the side shaving heads during the set.

8.

Biafra remembers this differently: "He [Gilliam] never mentioned the *Deaf Club* album to me. I thought I was the one who gave it to him. He told me he'd heard 'California Über Alles' on John Peel. He called up Peel to find out who put it out. When Peel said Alternative Tentacles, he said, 'that's it, I've got to find this band.'"

9.

The song would inspire a 1998 novel written by Joel Rose, concerning the fight for survival in a building located in Manhattan's Lower East Side as gentrification loomed on the horizon. Originally serialised in magazine form, it in turn became the basis for a 2001 screenplay, produced by John Malkovich's Mr Mudd Productions and directed by *Sopranos* and *Homicide* veteran Alan Taylor, which retained the title. "I was a fan and the song was in the wind," confirms Rose, "and it kept on playing in my head, and it seemed to me I didn't have to think twice, there was no choice. It was insistent and perfect, it was the title, there was never anything else."

10.

This is one side of the lopsided credit-staking that results in the mutual distrust and recriminations that have simmered through the years. Another tangential point is that the source of Ray and Klaus's inventiveness – a knowledge of and ability to draw on a host of musical traditions and styles – comes hand in glove with a reverence for rock 'n' roll tradition. Whereas Biafra was very much, philosophically at least, a child of punk rock – believing that it represented more than just a momentary deviation from the rock 'n' roll circus.

Punk ethics dictate suspicion of any kind of careerism. And it's hard to dispute the fact that Ray and Klaus *did* harbour ambitions to push the band into the same kind of stratosphere as – let's pick The Clash as an obvious example. They wanted the concomitant rewards they felt they'd earned. Biafra's politics and moral compass were always going to be a bulwark against that and in retrospect you can see why the relationship became fraught, even at the outset. The authorship claims can't be reconciled here, but they essentially amount to Biafra stating that most of the musical ideas for the songs as well as the lyrics were his. And he will point to the plethora of post-DKs recordings he has made, and the paucity of same originating from Ray and Klaus, as evidence of that. In the other corner Ray and Klaus argue that Biafra is a non-musician, which of itself makes the claim to *writing* music ridiculous. While your author does not doubt that Biafra was the main authorial and conceptual force behind the songwriting, underselling the massive contribution made by all three musicians to *Fresh Fruit*, even if Biafra feels justified due to their subsequent actions, is somewhat ungracious. There, I've said it. I've tucked it away in the footnotes like the big coward I am. Yours. A. Ogg, Dead Kennedys Truth and Reconciliation Committee, *retired*.

"I have *never* put them down as weak or talentless musicians," Biafra protests, hauling me back from garden leave. "They are far from it. I would never do that. But just because someone comes up with cool bass and drum fills does not mean they wrote the damn song. The melodies and arrangement did not come out of their heads. Sure, the whole was greater than the sum of the parts, and a lot of my favourite songs had more than one writer. But I am so sick of these greed-addled clowns claiming equal credit for unequal work."

He continues, in relation to the charge of 'non-musicianship'. "I could pick out the notes on a guitar, bass or even a keyboard when I had to. I am not the only 'non-musician' who composes with my voice – George Clinton, Captain Beefheart, Gary Floyd and even Charlie Chaplin for a full orchestra come to mind. I really do bring in entire songs, right down to the guitar solos. Another musician who's worked with Ray put it best when he said that what they are trying to do to me is like a secretary who typed a manuscript or took dictation turning around twenty years later and claiming they wrote the whole book."

He would also like to point out, for the record (in every sense), that "Not only do they now list D.H. Peligro as a co-writer of all the *Fresh Fruit* songs, and not Bruce [Ted], but Ray has now stripped Norm's production credit and substituted himself. If only you knew how frustrating it was for me to disappear to Colorado for a month or more to get away from the bullshit so I could write songs, come back with eight to twelve or so and find they had come up with absolutely nothing. Nada! If they really feel they came up with all the cool riffs, then why haven't they come up with any more? They've had twenty-five years and almost a decade of fake reunion shows, and how many new songs have they done? Ungracious? I never thought I would find myself being backed into a corner having to fight fire with fire against such chronic liars."

11.

In fact, the phrase 'God Told Me To Skin You Alive' would have a significant after-life. It was the title Winston Smith gave to his artwork for Green Day's *Insomniac* album, sneakily getting Biafra's most notorious lyric to number two in the American album charts. Or sometimes dissemination could arise from accident rather than design. Two years earlier, in 1993, a Baptist broadcaster called one thousand radio stations frantically urging them not to broadcast their weekly syndicated Powerline programme. They had inadvertently sent copies of *Fresh Fruit* to some thirty stations – mis-labelled 'Baptist' – instead of the usual 'inspirational music'. "It's one of those unfortunate things that happens when human beings get involved," stated Richard McCartney, vice president of the Southern Baptist Radio-TV Commission. "I don't know if any DKs actually went out over Baptist airwaves," says Biafra, "but I did read that all misprint copies were recalled by the pressing plant and burned in front of some ministers to keep them falling into the hands of people like . . . me."

12.

The original cassette version of the album contained two extra tracks (the b-sides 'In-Sight' and 'Police Truck'), and most European copies added 'Too Drunk To Fuck' as a bonus vinyl cut. It should be noted that the original UK CD reissue was mastered from vinyl while all US reissues were cut from the original masters. A 'di-gipak' reissue was remastered from original tapes by Bernie Grundman and Biafra prior to Ray's 25th anniversary overhaul in 2005. There are some disputes as to which version sounds better.

13.

One of the problems that became obvious during the conduct of these exchanges was that there is a genuine clash in terms of political opinion between Ray and Biafra. To some extent, I have sympathies for Ray's position. And to that end I incorporate some of our conversation below. It might not add much to discussion of either Dead Kennedys or *Fresh Fruit*'s legacy, and it's been dated by subsequent events, but it does reveal that Biafra was far from the only person in the band thinking through these issues. I also have to say that Ray was absolutely vocal – and informed – about the politics of pragmatism.

"Like I say, we have lots of Green Party here [in San Francisco]. I live two blocks from Berkeley, California, one of the most liberal spots. I was able to convince some people but it's like – 'Bush and Gore are the same'. I said – I disagree. That's an easy, easy line. There are a lot of similarities. But think about who will appoint the supreme court justices. What I found out was that women were much more open to that argument than men, because it's a freedom of choice issue. The men – 'No, they're all the same'. The women I could convince. You may think they're the same, but who's going to appoint supreme court justices that will protect your rights? And the light bulb went on. But Bush won, and here we are. The one thing people don't realise is, it's easy to slip into a right-wing thing when you have an outside enemy. Every dictator justifies what they're doing because it's 'for the good of the country'. Pinochet in Chile, he doesn't think he was oppressing people. He thinks he was saving them from themselves. The same thing in the US. The right wing doesn't think they're oppressing people – they're saving us."

That was the thing that DKs particularly attacked throughout their career – I was reading Klaus's stuff on going on the wedge issues – letting people scrap over something that will divide them while a bulldozer is driven through your civil rights.

"Exactly. The real thing that's happening over here is that wealth is being transferred from the middle and working class to the rich class. It's getting to be a banana republic. A hundred rich families at the top, minuscule middle class and a huge amount of poor at the bottom. In Guatemala, the rich family has to have defences around your house and guards. It's just un-Christian! One of the things it says in the Bible is take care of the poor. Where's that in all these family value issues? The hypocrisy is . . . you have to have a sense of humour, or it would be depressing. You have to remind people that Hitler in Germany didn't coerce people to follow him, he persuaded them. Everybody has a dark side and a good side. It's what you call upon, that makes the difference between a great leader and an evil leader – what do you appeal to in people . . . Karl Rove is a genius. But I don't think he really CARES about America, he just cares about getting his way. If the electorate is not educated, that's not my fault, but I'm going to take advantage of it. He's said that in interviews. What happened to – ask not what your country can do for you, ask what you can do for your country? What happened to that? A country is a community . . . The free market doesn't exist. It's a myth. The government always has to regulate the market. And to say government regulation is evil is a lie. We'll have an earthquake in California, and one or two people die. An earthquake in a Central American country, and 4,000 people die. Because they don't have any building codes. Everyone loves to whine about the government, but you should go some place that doesn't have one."

14.

"I didn't write much on the Dead Kennedys and the couple or so short reviews I did write were unfavourable," confirms Jared Johnson, who retired from rock criticism to write the *Denver Post*'s bridge column. "I remember back then I did an entire column on just weird punk rock names I compiled going through the bins of local record store, Wax Trax, that carried *everything*. Either my lead or my conclusion was that 'Most punk rock groups exhausted their creativity coming up with their names'. [This ran a few years later, after his original condemnation of DKs.] I really don't remember much about the Dead Kennedys' music except that even with 'punk rock' I still wanted a bit more melodicism with my music. I remember the DKs had some interesting covers, including one that featured one of those smiley face water towers (the rear cover of *Plastic Surgery Disasters*), that I actually came across (I think it was the same one) about a quarter century later driving south-east out of Chicago toward Indianapolis. I spent hours taking pictures of it from all angles!"

Right: Winston Smith's collage entitled *God Told Me to Skin You Alive* – after Biafra's opening lyric to 'I Kill Children' – was recreated as a fold-out poster for the Green Day album *Insomniac*, 1995.

BE SAFE IN THE 80'S

DO NOT:
UNDER ANY CIRCUMSTANCES

THIS COULD BE YOU!

1. CRITICIZE THE NEW REGIME
2. QUIT YOUR JOB
3. DRESS FUNNY
4. BE SEEN WITH ANYONE CONSIDERED STRANGE
5. QUESTION AUTHORITY
6. OBJECT TO BEING RELIEVED OF YOUR RIGHTS
7. RESIST FIGHTING A WAR FOR CORPORATE INTERESTS
8. GIVE IN TO THE URGE TO REBEL
9. ADMIT THAT ANYTHING IS WRONG
10. THINK FOR YOURSELF

DON'T TAKE RISKS!

The Kooties
LENNY
AND THE
SPITWADS
THE CLIP-ONS
&
HALF-LIFE
now at ROOM 101
$3.00 AT THE DOOR

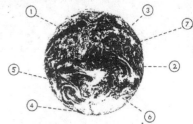

COLLATERAL DAMAGE

"IT IS BY THE FORCE OF IMAGES
THAT, IN THE COURSE OF TIME,
REAL REVOLUTIONS ARE MADE."
            -- ANDRÉ BRETON

FALLOUT EDITORS

Aaron Blurr
      Navigation
Zeno Weevil
      Observation
Krass Vermin
      Agitation
Ray Vaughn
      Polemic
Koda Chrome
      Sympathy
Winston Smith
      Antipathy
Rangoon Dandy
      Sarcasm
355
      Vibes

PERFECTION

DISPOSABLE
WASTE

Editorial Staff in a relaxed moment

"We surrealists are alergic
to things as they are"

FALLOUT #3 PUBLISHED IN NOV. 1980
#4 PUBLISHED IN MARCH, 1981

THE FALLOUT TIME CAPSULE

NO TURNING BACK

MORE MONEY   NEW CAREER

1980 1981 **1982** 1983

1984 **2000**

1999

1985 1998

1986

1987 **1997**

1988 1996

1989 1995

1990

1991 1993

1992 1994

☆MILLENNIUM MADNESS!

POWER   LASER

ZAP   LASER X-SOURCE

SPud

HIGH EXPLOSIVES   DANGEROUS

In a fit of civic altruism we are compiling a list of goodies to leave as a momento to the future (if there is to be a future) and we invite you to participate. Fill in the coupon below & send us your entry. The lucky winners will each recieve a 1981 Fallout Calendar of Xerox Art. The only calendar with THIRTEEN months. 20 items will be included, one for each remaining year of the 20th century. (By the way, 20 years is the average life span of a nuclear waste container, even if the contents DO last half a million years longer...) So, if there's anything you'd like to leave for your descendants besides plutonium, now's your chance. Contest results will be published in the next issue of FALLOUT.

Mail to:

FALLOUT
PRODUCTIONS
355
CA.

1981 TIME CAPSULE
List your entry below

X_____

20 entries will be selected. Winners will be notified by mail.

Name_____
Address_____
City_____
State_____ Zip_____
■ Deadline: March 15, 1981

GRAFIC ANARCHY

As it must be obvious, we do not have a typesetter, we can't spell, we lack even a rudimentary english vocabulary, and we can't draw two parallel lines. But that hasn't stopped us so far.
The way we look at it, there's more to life than marketable technical skills. While two thirds of the world is starving the remaining third is at home watching performing beasts on television or busy selling inflatable party dolls door to door. Isn't it time for a change?

Our aim is to provide a forum for ideas and images from the surrealist's point of view. Satire and humor are essentials. Our emphasis on anti-nuclear issues and topics regarding our civil liberties is a general theme but by no means the constant rule.

We solicit any related artwork, manuscripts, poetry, etc. that you may wish to submit. DON'T send any originals of anything. And unless you include a self addressed stamped envelope don't expect to see it again.

Send all submissions to FALLOUT P.O. Box 355 California

IN THE NEXT ISSUE:

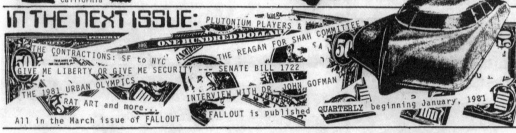

PLUTONIUM PLAYERS &
THE CONTRACTIONS: SF to NYC
GIVE ME LIBERTY OR GIVE ME SECURITY --- SENATE BILL 1722
THE REAGAN FOR SHAH COMMITTEE
THE 1981 URBAN OLYMPICS
INTERVIEW WITH DR. JOHN GOFMAN
RAT ART and more...
FALLOUT is published QUARTERLY beginning January, 1981
All in the March issue of FALLOUT

𝔇𝔢𝔞𝔡 𝔎𝔢𝔫𝔫𝔢𝔡𝔶𝔰

The Story of Fresh Fruit
For Rotting Vegetables

Yakety Yak

"We have a sense of humour and we're not afraid to use it in a vicious way if we have to. In some ways, we're cultural terrorists, using music instead of guns."
Jello Biafra, quoted in *Forced Exposure* #4

Interviewer: "Isn't a Dead Kennedys concert on Nov 22 [anniversary of JFK assassination] in bad taste?"
East Bay Ray: "Of course. But the assassinations weren't too tasteful either."
East Bay Ray, November 22, 1979, interviewed by the *Vancouver Sun*

"People should take things rock stars say with a grain of salt, because there's no one in rock and roll right now who's a relevant example of a spokesperson for anything. They do have an influence on people, and I think there's a new consciousness that's really positive among rock stars, like Rock the Vote. They're trying to make people aware, but I really can't think of anyone who's really schooled enough to be political to the point that would be required for a rock star. If Jello Biafra was a big international star, it would be really cool. But he's not on a major label, and he doesn't write commercial enough music to use that as a tool."
Kurt Cobain, Nirvana, speaking in 1990

"Biafra takes on the monied classes and the government, and the songs become almost too intricate for punk. Massively influential."
Alternative Press's **10 Essential Political-Revolution Albums**

Left: Page from *Fallout* #3, November 1980, by Winston Smith – "The advert for 'Kill The Poor' came from a collage I made around 1968 from a bunch of old upper-crust art mags from the 1920s. Even the original 'shadow lettering' came from a book on type styles I bought in 1962 with a two dollar bill my granny gave me for my birthday."

"My favourite tour bus activity? Probably getting drunk, listening to Dead Kennedys and beating Mitch, our tour manager, up." . . . "My education was punk rock – what the Dead Kennedys said, what Operation Ivy said. It was attacking America, but it was American at the same time."
Billie Joe Armstrong of Green Day

"God bless Jello!"
Elijah Wood, actor

"The band grew up heavily influenced by both the metal and the punk scene and in particular, the Bay Area punk scene, bands like Attitude Adjustment and Dead Kennedys."
Rob Flynn, Machine Head

"What is a 'real punk'? Somebody who lives according to the 'No future' slogan? Punk for us is a musical category, which means a sound with tempo and huge amounts of energy. We were inspired by bands such as the Dead Kennedys and T.S.O.L. We do think about our future, we even think about what will happen after The Offspring. I doubt we'll be around as long as The Rolling Stones . . . Fuck the people who say I'm not punk. I was beaten by the cops at a Dead Kennedys show."
Dexter Holland, The Offspring

"The fast stuff got meteoric, and the slower stuff got less important."
Grant Hart, Hüsker Dü, talking to Michael Azerrad about the DKs' influence

"The first time I heard 'Holiday In Cambodia' I was probably 14 years old, and I heard it on the radio, college radio in Massachusetts. It just sounded so psychedelic, and powerful and noisy and angry. I was totally transfixed. I'd never heard anything like it. It was like Jimi Hendrix, but way better . . . It was just so exciting. Hearing that song for the first time was a real peak for me. Just walking into my room and hearing that song, standing in the doorway = what is this? And looking round the room as if the sound was coming from the corners of the room rather than the speakers . . . What I really liked about it was the guitar, but also at the core of it is this raging anger, really articulate as well. It's a song that just kept revealing itself to me when I bought the record. I listened to it all the time trying to figure out how that happened. Every time I was just amazed by it."
Lou Barlow, Dinosaur Jr., Sebadoh, on his all-time favourite record

"[They] really influenced me a lot, still to this day, getting me to question what the government is up to and question sort of blind consumerism and things like that."
Shepard Fairey, graphic artist/originator of the Barack Obama 'Hope' poster

"I was also into bands like Dead Kennedys, Sex Pistols, Black Flag, The Clash, a lot of those bands were influences on thrash metal, and we're in the epicenter of where it started, well in LA and up north in the Bay Area."
David Ellefson, Megadeth

"It's [punk] just starting to happen in America, but of course not with the same venom, and there's quite an interesting band called the Dead Kennedys, who've got the same kind of venom as the Sex Pistols."
Pete Townshend (he actually said "but none of the genius", but we disagree)

"Punk rock had this cool, political, personal message. You know what I mean? It was a lot more cerebral than stupid cock rock. Dead Kennedys, MDC . . . remember?"
Krist Novoselic, Nirvana

"While touring in San Francisco and playing the Mabuhay Gardens, we saw Jello Biafra in a restaurant. We went in and sat down at his table and immediately started eating his food. He didn't seem to mind."
Henry Rollins, Black Flag etc.

". . . other bands that we like and cherish [are] such as Turbonegro, Electric Frankenstein, Dead Kennedys and Zeke."
Howlin' Pelle Almqvist, The Hives

"Dead Kennedys could echo both the weirdness of Beefheart and the sort of spectral pop that came off Spector's production line. Still fresh. No rot."
***Uncut* magazine**

"When the Dead Kennedys started, people in the scene didn't just like them because they were a 'guitar band'. People liked them because they were very creative and original and funny, from their 'anti-fashion' down to their lyrics. Not only was Jello very political, he also had the ability to break down preconceived notions of the front-man formula and the audience/performer relationship. We could share a bill

with them at that time because people weren't looking for 'punk uniforms' . . . people in the scene were looking for craziness and business-as-*un*usual."
Scott Ryser, The Units (in discussion with John Doran)

"Jello Biafra is America's Morrissey."
Grant Young, Soul Asylum (and you can make of this what you will. "Morrissey?" interjects Biafra. "Oh, gawd . . .")

"The Dead Kennedys are the band that made us see the world in a whole new depressing way."
Stza, Leftöver Crack

"By age twelve I indulged my every thought into the punk scene and grew up with the writings of Jello Biafra of DK and Dick from Subhumans."
Mike Voss, aka House DJ 007

"I wanted to do something that people who are into bands would like. Jello Biafra was a big influence."
Wil Hodgson, Perrier-winning stand-up comic

"Then I got more into East Bay Ray from Dead Kennedys and Greg Ginn from Black Flag. I really liked their styles."
Bill Kelliher, Mastodon

"Why does it matter? Because they alone got me through school days, *Fresh Fruit*'s cathartic release every morn and night; the anthems of liberation gave credence to the outsider, thrilled with their active incitement to rebel."
Owen Adams, *The Guardian*

"I was only fifteen years old when I encountered this album; its black sense of humour (poison gas, child murder) coupled with a puzzling image of a lounge band emblazoned with DK logos confused me somewhat. Over time I gradually began to realise that what I was really grappling with wasn't just a bunch of quirky songs and images but a massive sense of irony and an off-the-radar level of intelligence. Having figured out that the 'The Sounds of Sunshine' actually had minimal involvement with either 'punk rock' or the images of San Francisco's 'White Night

Riots', I found a belated endorsement of Picasso's line 'art is a lie that tells the truth'. You live and learn."
Andy Higgins, Just Say No To Government Music

"I was at eleven or twelve years old living in Atlanta, Georgia. This radio station – 88.5 – they had this show that played everything from Misfits to Dead Kennedys to Animosity to Corrosion of Conformity, Agnostic Front, Slayer, and just all these bands. I just started making tapes right off the radio. I still have 'em to this day. That is what officially changed me, and introduced me to a whole new world."
Hank Williams III

"I was all about the Motown stuff. Otis Redding, Al Green, etc. I also listened to Dead Kennedys, Joy Division, Bauhaus, Fishbone, and Jane's Addiction."
Matt Noveskey, Blue October

"A lot looser and more atmospheric than some of their later songs."
Moby, on 'Holiday In Cambodia', one of his twenty favourite punk discs

"When Kerry [King] and I met, he was into Priest, Maiden, AC/DC and stuff like that. I was just getting out of that, getting into punk. So, I knew what he was listening to, but he didn't know what I was listening to. He was like 'What the hell is this?' 'It's punk, man. Dead Kennedys! It's great!' The speed part of the band basically came from me listening to punk and then getting Dave [Lombardo] into it, because Dave loved it."
Jeff Hanneman, Slayer

I grew up with the second and third wave of Punk. My first two records were The Cure's *Concert* and the Dead Kennedys' *Fresh Fruit For Rotting Vegetables*.
Damian Monzillo, hair stylist to the stars

"I have a very sad story to tell about the first punk rock show I ever wanted to go to. It was the Dead Kennedys, and I had just gotten my driver's licence the day before. I wanted to drive there really bad but my parents said, 'No, you can't take the car. It's in a bad area and it's too late.' I really wanted to go and I threw a temper tantrum. I got so angry that they wouldn't let me go with anyone else 'cause I was being such a brat."
Stephen Malkmus, Pavement (in conversation with Jason Fine)

Gene: "The best punk rock bands don't ever take a lead. I don't listen to punk rock that's got solos." Dean: "Unless it's East Bay Ray of the Dead Kennedys. But then he was a whole different thing."
Gene and Dean Ween

"What the hell happened to the revolutionary attitude in music? You can't find it anywhere. I know. I looked. Is it just a coincidence that bands that talk about it have been silenced from the mainstream? I think not. Where's the next Bob Marley, Public Enemy, KRS-ONE, Bad Brains, Dead Kennedys or Cro-Mags?"
John Joseph, Cro-Mags

"Jello Biafra has to be one of the best front-men we know of. Every lyric is sung with such conviction."
Rise Against

"I've got plenty of both Jethro Tull *and* the Dead Kennedys *and* N.W.A, which is pretty normal these days. I think when it comes to music most people do tend to listen to everything and not be as clique-y."
Jeffrey Lewis, folk singer (in conversation with Mairi Mackay)

"When I was a kid, the underground scene was so underground. The radio was all funk radio stations playing Kraftwerk and Sugarhill Gang and we were just measly little punks that liked Black Flag and the Dead Kennedys."
Pepper, Corrosion of Conformity

"Back in the early days of Portland punk rock the DKs, like the rest of us, didn't have very many venues to play so they were forced to take their band on the road, which was to travel up and down the I-5 [Interstate]. Even in doing that there still wasn't many places to play. Dead Kennedys liked to play in Portland because we had one of the few punk scenes that was organised enough to have consistently good venues and attendance for every show they played, and that was true for other bands that we booked as well. DKs were easy to work with and always put on a great show. Everyone looked forward to having them come to town."
Dave Corboy, Sado-Nation

"I mean, The Dead Kennedys? I was at the Roundhouse and they were all watching television and one of them came up to me and said what a big fan he was . . ."
It wasn't Jello Biafra was it?
"Dunno, mate. I wouldn't know one Dead Kennedy from another."
Phil Collins, in conversation with the late Steven Wells ("It definitely wasn't *me*". **Biafra**)

"*Fresh Fruit* was my *Never Mind The Bollocks*".
Kenny Helwig, Breakdown, Slip, Forgotten etc.

"The main punk influences for myself was The Misfits and the Dead Kennedys, they were huge influences on me."
Scott Crouse, Earth Crisis

"Biafra has been consistent in his values since the day I met him and a lifelong influence on me. We've had some amazing times, especially a few years ago when he and I travelled by train [he likes travelling on trains] on his spoken word tour. At one point he was told off by an old lady for nudging her feet under the table. If only she knew! Biafra once described me as his old friend. I am, and he is mine."
Mick McGee, former DKs roadie

"I saw them in late 1979 when they opened for The Clash . . . Jello Biafra ended up in the crowd, after which he was pretty much naked, his clothes being ripped off by the rabid fans."
Steven Rubio, writer

"For example, if the celebrity I selected was Jello Biafra, I could either mimic singing a Dead Kennedys song, or I could say 'my first name sounds like a dessert treat.'"
WikiHow entry on 'How to Play the Party Game Celebrity'

"Forget the Sex Pistols, forget The Clash, the Dead Kennedys were unquestionably the best punk band ever. As offensive and aggressive as Eminem, the Pistols and Amen put together and as intelligent, purposeful and passionate as Public Enemy, Godspeed and Radiohead."
Ben Haggar, journalist

"Awesome"
Colin Lambert, pro-skateboarder (who uses 'California Über Alles' to theme his YouTube clips)

"When the Dead Kennedys came to DC, I thought, 'I have to go.' When I saw them I was way up front, and all these people were constantly jumping off the stage, five at a time. The club was so packed that these waves of people were jumping into the crowd like it was an ocean. I just sort of stood next to the wall thinking, 'What the fuck?'"
Joe Lally, Fugazi

"Singer Jello Biafra's vitriolic, merciless verbal lambasting set to a musical backdrop of fervid punk."
***Mojo*'s Top 50 Punk Albums**

"We listened to a lot of CDs (to avert tour boredom), Metallica, Black Sabbath, Dead Kennedys, the Ramones."
Jesse Colburn, Avril Lavigne's former beau and guitarist

"When I was a teenager, I was a kind of rebellious skateboarder. Dead Kennedys were a big influence, they were my big band. Some friends and I also formed a little band. We never did anything proper, but that was my start to music."
Skyler Taugher, techno fusionists Shdwplay

". . . a highlight of one of the most seminal punk albums, and one of the all-time best punk songs, no question."
Louis Pattison, NME, on 'California Über Alles'

"There's a lot of good stuff out there and it wouldn't be fair to pick one over all other. But personally I like the Dead Kennedys, Bad Brains, the punk angle."
Shavo Odadjian, System of a Down

"One of the finest slabs of rant 'n' roll ever made."
Kerrang!

"One of the most fiery, politically explosive diatribes you are ever likely to hear . . ."
***Q Magazine*'s 100 Best Punk Albums**

"It was obvious that they weren't just another band that was gonna come and go. They were something special. Biafra was an absolute talent. And he had a band behind him that were tight and good."
Howie Klein, quoted in *Gimme Something Better*

"No-one around me seemed to be constantly horrified by the casual callousness and brutality that passed for school-life. Or disgusted by the bizarre social-hierarchies everywhere. Or terrified at the prospect of having to go murder forty or so years of life in an office, just to secure yourself a big screen TV and a boat. But finally, here, on this tape, was someone saying, 'Yes, this society we've built is crazy, and ugly, and wrong, but we could do whole a lot better if we just grew-up and tried.' It was, and is, an inspiring message."
Nick Sheehan, Grease Trap Blog, on Dead Kennedys

"I went pretty much [to the DKs Rock Against Reagan show in Washington] for the reason that the Dead Kennedys were playing and at the time they were one of my favourite bands. I remember Biafra staring up at the Washington Monument and calling it the 'Great Eternal Klansman with the two blinking red eyes.' There were police helicopters all over the place and buses filled up with riot police. As a thirteen-year-old kid, that was like my own little revolution."
Dave Grohl, Scream, Nirvana, Foo Fighters etc., interviewed in *Dance Of Days*

"One day, this kid Eric from my Social Studies class brought in a cassette tape of the Dead Kennedys' *Fresh Fruit For Rotting Vegetables* and I listened to it and my life was changed completely. Just hearing the sarcastic, but catchy early Dead Kennedys stuff just wowed me."
Adam Gierasch, horror film director

"The sound of the West Coast hardcore scene they joined has sometimes been stereotyped as regimentally fast, loud and simple, the uniform product of gangs of impatient upstart youths chewing away at punk's already thin margin of musical subtlety. If this was true (even if), Dead Kennedys would be the one great shining exception."
Jack Davies, The Quietus

"Dead Kennedys brought a horror-show vibe to punk that remains more unsettling than the Misfits' comic-book core and battier than My Chemical Romance's make-up."
Magnet

"Jello's kind of like my weird, retarded uncle. He's part of the family. [We met] twenty-seven years ago in Chicago, I went backstage, and we didn't have sex. I wasn't a groupie. But we talked for a while. I thought he was an idiot. He thought I was an idiot. And we got along ever since."
Al Jourgensen, Ministry, talking to Pitchfork in 2008

"*Fresh Fruit* scans like an old anarchist newspaper. But 'Kill the Poor' sounds perfect for Dick Cheney's America."
***Spin* magazine, 50 Most Essential Punk Records**

"America's answer to the Sex Pistols – singer Jello Biafra sounded like Johnny Rotten on helium – Dead Kennedys assaulted religion, capitalism, and the government with a double dose of rage and humour. 'Kill the Poor,' 'Holiday in Cambodia' and 'Let's Lynch the Landlord' are just some of the rapid-fire highlights of their influential 1980 debut."
Dan Epstein, *Revolver* magazine's 50 Greatest Punk Albums of All Time

"Jello and I go way back. He helped the Hüskers get their first gigs in San Francisco, and Alternative Tentacles put out the first Hüskers album in the UK. [On introducing Biafra to John Lydon] It was funny watching those two meet for the first time . . . It was great; a real meeting of the minds. I got out of there as soon as possible because if I had stayed, I wouldn't have been able to get a word in edgewise with those two."
Bob Mould of **Hüsker Dü, Sugar etc.,** talking to Mark Kemp of *Option* magazine in 1991

"Music is more difficult – try naming a political band. The Dead Kennedys. The Dead Kennedys are political, but they are more funny than they are political."
Thom Yorke of **Radiohead**

"One of my favourite rock 'n' roll memories is of an after-party during the DKs' first visit to Seattle. Recognise that bands like this for me – these actual guys being at a

party in the SAME HOUSE that I was in – was like being in the presence of Led Zeppelin or Kiss."
Duff McKagan, Guns N' Roses

"Frantic music is good, like with Discharge and all those early punk bands. But it was with the Dead Kennedys that things got a lot more interesting – not just a bombardment of sound but an interesting production as well."
Massive Attack

A Look at What's Ahead

THE
REAGAN FUTURE

Pattern of things to come

San Francisco Chronimer

The Invisible Solution

EVERY HOUR ★★★★ EVERY DAY... *get relief the instant way!* NOSE PADS MADE IN HAITI

THE WORLD OF TOMORROW
expiring in 1984

Is *Our presidential puppet*
SCHIZOPHRENIC?

Oregon bombs Nevada

What Subjects Are
Best to Avoid?

Rat Cuts Off Electricity

Rats Invading
POLICE
BATTLE RATS

Rats Fled

Rats Ratify

19-Hour Rampage

Sex Scandal

REAGAN UNVEILS NEW PRESIDENTIAL LOGO

The Double 'R' Brand

President Reagan today displayed the new Presidential Insignia. The logo will be issued to all Party Officials, Government workers, the Armed Forces, and Consumer/Citizens in the form of Tee shirts, arm bands, and tattoos.

All My Friends
Are Going to Be
Rat-Catchers

They slept 25,136 hours

Possible Sex Motive
when you brush your teeth!

" Wet Rat's **Doomsday Powder**

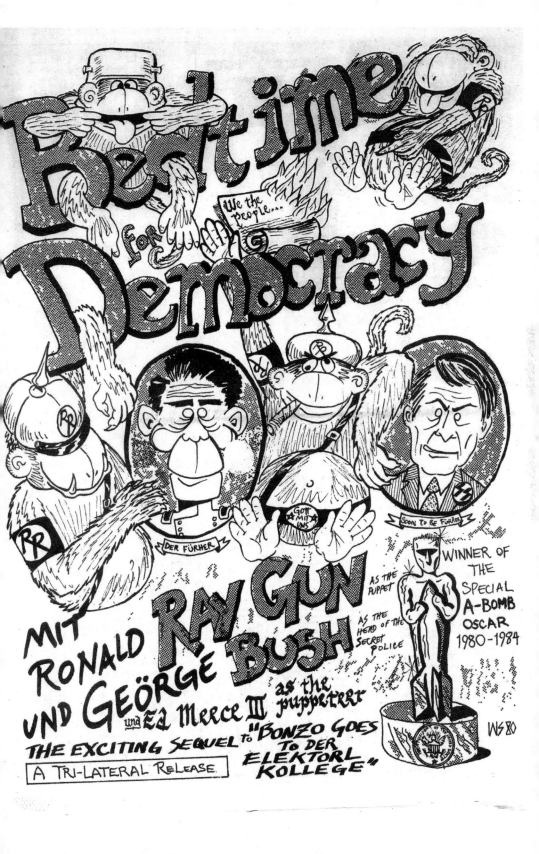

PRAYER

O Sacred Gridd,

Protector of the Realm of Non-reality,

Defender of the Faith Dubious,

Keeper of the Status Quo,

Saviour of the Bourgeoisie;

We come before Thee in this hour with mixed pivots

and humbly do we employ Thee and ask Thy remittence

for those deeds done in Denver and in the heat of Venice.

Betray us the Bombdeath Eternal,

Protect us from Evil Knievil,

and deliver us from the fall of the colbolt.

Further, O Faithful Gourd,

We compose to petrify our existance in Thee

and to perpetuate without reason

as will be Thy folly.

Gerd over all those in deed

and deliver us from Immaculate Perception.

All this do we compromise

In Ford's Name

Amend.

Blessed are the Simple-minded
    for they shall be fleeced

  Blessed are the Vidiots
      for they shall be led by the nose

    Blessed are the Cloven Hooved
        for they shall be in good company

     Blessed are the Schizophrenic
         for they shall know no loneliness

      Blessed are the Mono-minds
          for they not stray from the program

       Blessed are the Pin Heads
           for they shall lead the masses

        Blessed are the Clones
            for they shall multiply,
              add, subtract, & devide

         Blessed are the Hemopheliacs
             for they shall not bleed

          Blessed are the Stocks & Bonds
              for they shall be called "High Risk"

           Blessed are the Credit Slaves
               for they shall say "Charge It!"

𝔊𝔯𝔞𝔣𝔦𝔠 𝔄𝔫𝔞𝔯𝔠𝔥𝔶

Winston Smith — All
Art Is Propaganda

I n 1976, upon returning from a seven-year absence studying classical art in Italy, the Oklahoma-born artist that would become known as Winston Smith legally assumed the name of George Orwell's protagonist (from his classic 1948 novel *Nineteen Eighty-Four*) as a direct response to the striking changes he observed in American society. As Smith recalls, "I hitchhiked across the country in March of 1976 and arrived in San Francisco on Saint Patrick's Day (which, believe-you-me, was one hell of a welcoming party!)." Initially, he worked as a roadie for a couple of years, where he was to encounter the nascent punk scene first-hand. "I recall my first inklings of awareness of that scene, when a band called 'Television' came through our studios and a local performer named Mary Monday rehearsed there. Then my awareness grew of the Stranglers and then the Sex Pistols, etc. And it's been all downhill since then."

At that point, the US West Coast punk subculture was very art-based, employing a whole gamut of strategies ranging from performance, film, photography and visual arts to music and fashion. Smith's early contribution to the scene began with the creation of spoof flyers for fictitious gigs, often utilising found photographs and illustrations taken from advertising and the news media, and particularly archive images used to promote the 'American dream' of '50s consumerism. The names of performers and venues on these flyers were dreamt up by Smith himself – groups such as Lenny and the Spitwads, the Rejex or Idiot Child "performing live at the Orb" or at other fictitious clubs such as Nico's and Room 101 – names that were close enough to the conventions of the growing scene to sound realistic, with convincing graphic treatments to match. Some of these names arose directly from Smith's own reflections on contemporary issues. "Another fake band name I made up was 'Anonymous Technicians'. That name came to me after reading an article in 1978 about a new plan they had for executing people. Instead of hanging, firing squad or electrocution, they were proposing 'death by chemical injection administered by anonymous technicians.' Now that is the norm."

Smith soon formed a partnership with fellow artist Jayed Scotti (later of Feederz), producing the self-published magazine *Fallout* from 1978 onwards. This 11 x 17 inch newsprint publication provided a vehicle for bringing together various parts of their practice – including spoof flyers, politically-charged essays, barbed comments and original collage and illustration material that was to later reappear on some of the record sleeves of Dead Kennedys and other Alternative Tentacles label releases. Smith also 'created' a number of other fictitious contributors to *Fallout*, extending the editorial 'team' to a group of seven (including the wonderfully-monickered Zeno Weevil, Krass Vermin and Rangoon Dandy – even Smith's cat, 355, got a name-check).

The combination of offbeat, surreal practical-jokery, combined with disturbing and hard-hitting satire in Smith's work found a common accord with Jello Biafra. During the early development of Dead Kennedys, Biafra had been working with visual material along similar lines, collecting images from popular magazines and newspapers along with headlines and commentary that could be re-positioned in order to question and undermine the original message. Both Biafra and Smith recognised the potential for their visual compositions to amuse and shock through the employment of heavily ironic and disturbing graphic humour. Such strategies were not new, of course – European Dada artists in the early twentieth century had used collage techniques to critique the horrors of World War I and the subsequent collapse of the Weimar Republic. Notable exponents of political critique through the discordant juxtaposition of found imagery included Raoul Hausmann and Hannah Höch, while John Heartfield's experiments with photomontage were to reach a worldwide audience in the '30s as the artist fled the Nazi regime and developed a sophisticated visual response to the horrors that beset Germany in the lead-up to World War II. Such precursors, along with the radical politics of the early surrealists led by André Breton, were to directly inform the founders of the Situationist International in the early '60s. Especially relevant to the field of visual communication was the situationist notion of 'détournement' – whereby a visual message could be disarmed or corrupted through its combination or juxtaposition with alternative texts or other visual elements.

The apotheosis of the strategy of détournement wasn't to come, however, until some time later, when the punk movement spawned a graphic language that could reflect its critical and anti-authoritarian message in a direct and visceral manner. Jamie Reid's work for the Sex Pistols provided a clear lead in the UK, though he, in turn, had been working in a similar vein for some time with *Suburban Press* and had drawn extensively upon the heritage of graphic design activism and art practice. Gee Vaucher's self-initiated publication *International Anthem* adopted similar strategies, while her subsequent visual work with Crass took the technique further, moving away from more traditional collage to the creation of sophisticated illustrations that appeared initially to resemble photomontage, but were in fact hand-rendered.

Winston Smith, working both individually and in collaboration with Jello Biafra, was to become the US equivalent of these early punk graphic pioneers in the UK. Smith's approach to collage is astute, witty and sophisticated, with a keen eye for detail and a concern for composition and balance – together with a love of ironic humour and the power of graphic design to inform, persuade and provoke. Like other graphic auteurs – designers who choose to develop a personal visual critique of the world around them, rather than simply working to commercial briefs – Smith built an extensive portfolio of visual work that could be drawn upon when needed to fit the requirements of the job at hand. The overarching aesthetic of Smith's work in *Fallout* is rough and raw – photographic images are usually distressed to stark monotone and the cut-and-paste image construction is undisguised. Type is often either roughly cut from newspaper or magazine headlines, or simply hand-rendered in heavy black marker pen, with body text uniformly typewritten. The magazines were litho-printed, but retain some of the qualities of simple photocopying, very much in keeping with the generic punk fanzine style of the period.

Various examples of work that Smith published within the pages of *Fallout* in 1980-81 would see the light of day on record covers and flyers further down the line – even inspiring album titles such as the *Let Them Eat Jellybeans!* compilation and Dead Kennedys' 1986 final album, *Bedtime For Democracy*. One of Smith's most striking – and notorious – compositions, a three-dimensional crucifixion entitled 'Idol', based around a collage of dollar bills, was subsequently reproduced as a two-dimensional colour photocopy image and as part of another spread within the third issue of *Fallout* in November 1980. The image formed the central premise for the DKs' mini-album *In God We Trust, Inc.* in 1981, heightening both the group's and the artist's notoriety in the process. However, his most celebrated and enduring work was the design of Dead Kennedys' logo – a classic example of hard-edged, memorable, simple and direct graphic branding. The logo can be easily reproduced in its simplest form (a simple vertical line and cross to form the letters 'DK'), though Smith's original retains an element of apparent three-dimensionality through a clever use of line weight and tone.

Smith also designed the Alternative Tentacles logo, and recalls trekking across the city to the studio where the DKs were recording *Fresh Fruit* in order to deliver the artwork, where he also encountered the legendary Norm; "I personally met Norm the cat at Mobius Music. I had to hitchhike into San Francisco from my remote ranch and meet Biafra there to deliver to him the original for the Alternative Tentacles logo. When I got there he and the DKs were still recording, so I sat in the ante-chamber to wait. Norm the cat came and sat in my lap and after the band emerged from the recording booth Biafra was clearly tickled to introduce me to the cat and point out that he was being named as the 'Producer' of the new record. Nice cat. Very friendly. Excellent record producer – for someone without opposable thumbs."

Winston Smith's design legacy is far-reaching – his graphic style has been widely imitated across the punk and hardcore underground, with more recent album sleeves by other designers for the likes of Leftöver Crack and Anti-Flag continuing the tradition. In an age of increasingly 'life-like' visual sophistication and the abundance of seamless Photoshop retouching, the rawness and directness of Smith's work from over thirty years ago still cuts right to the bone.

Russ Bestley
Designer/Writer

Examples of artwork from *Fallout* #3, November 1980, and *Fallout* #4, March 1981, are reproduced on pages 5-7, 28-29, 44, 56, 90-91, 100-101, 115, 128, 130-132, 150-152, 162-164, 176-180, 192-194, and 199-201 of this book. Design by Winston Smith.

KNOW WHO YOU'RE FIGHTING FOR...

IF YOU LOVE YOUR CAR DIE FOR IT.

B-58

BUY WAR BONDS NOW

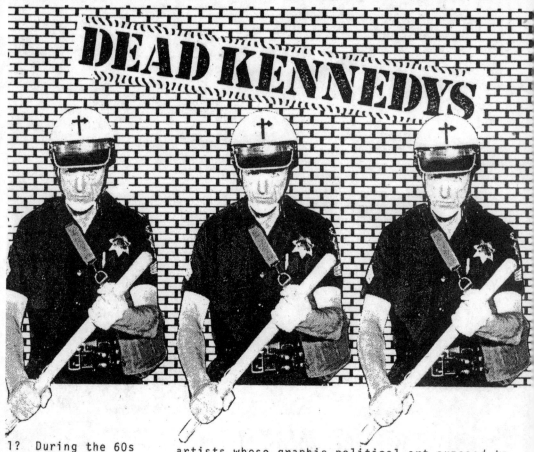

DEAD KENNEDYS

1? During the 60s protest songs with the modern equivaople will hear us. of Reagan's role as artists whose graphic political art exposed to the world the horrors of the Kaisar's butchery. Poets, artists, singers, both famous and unknown, along with countless peasant no-bodies have perished under fascist regimes for decades

ARE the CLOUDS LAUGHING AT YOU?

DON'T JUST STAND THERE, DO SOMETHING ABOUT IT! FIGHT BACK!

ADVERTISE IN FALLOUT

Page 8 Section C   April 13, 1980   S.F. Sunday Examiner & Chronicle

Plenty of fallout possible

Don't Let The Clouds Push You Around.

RATES	
FULL PAGE	$50
HALF PAGE	$30
QUARTER	$20
BACK PAGE	$75
CENTRE [2]	$90

ALL PRICES FOR CAMERA READY ART
DIMENTIONS: 10" x 14" for FULL PAGE

Fallout Design $30

FALLOUT PRODUCTIONS   355   CA.

Above: *In God We Trust, Inc.* – UK release 1981 (Statik) rear cover collage
Above: *In God We Trust, Inc.* – US release 1981 (Alternative Tentacles) promotional cover sticker
Above: *In God We Trust, Inc.* – Spanish release 1982 (Statik / Edigsa) promotional cover sticker
Above right: *In God We Trust, Inc.* – UK release 1981 (Statik)
Right: *In God We Trust, Inc.* – Label, Australian release 1981 (Missing Link) label
Far right: *In God We Trust, Inc.* – Label, Belgian release 1981 (Statik) label

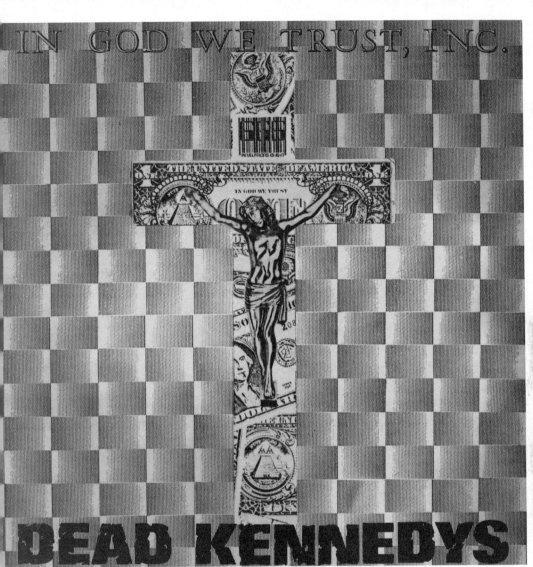

IN GOD WE TRUST, INC.

DEAD KENNEDYS

Above: 'Nazi Punks Fuck Off!' / 'Moral Majority' – US release 1981 (Alternative Tentacles)

About

Alex Ogg is an author and journalist specializing in music. His work has appeared in newspapers including *The Times* and *The Guardian*, numerous magazines, and websites. His books include *The Art of Punk* (an *Independent* newspaper book of the year 2012) with Dr. Russ Bestley, *Independence Days*, *No More Heroes*, and *The Hip Hop Years*. He is a regular speaker on TV, radio, and at literary events. He has lectured at several universities and currently edits the academic journal *Punk & Post-Punk*. He lives in London with his partner and two children.

Punk art surrealist **Winston Smith**, a master of "hand-carved" collage, has been crafting his thought-provoking art since the 1970s. Smith first became known for his collaborations with punk legends Dead Kennedys and his numerous album covers, inserts, and flyers for the band in their formative years. His technique of cutting out by hand and gluing each individual element has inspired a generation of artists. His published collections include *Act Like Nothing's Wrong*, *Artcrime*, and *All Riot on the Western Front*.

Born in New York, **Ruby Ray** migrated to San Francisco in the mid-1970s. She entered the underground scene while working at Tower Records in North Beach. When she acquired her first camera, she quickly turned it into a weapon. Ray shot using a Nikon FM and Tri-X 400 film, the fastest film of its time. While documenting new bands and people for *Search & Destroy* magazine, she wielded her lens like many young DIY artists were brandishing guitars—bold, carefree, and absolutely necessary. Ray's photos have been collected in the book *From the Edge of the World: California Punk, 1977–1981*.

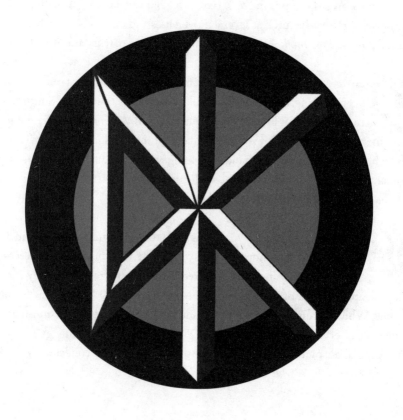

PM Press is an independent, radical publisher of critically necessary books for our tumultuous times. Our aim is to deliver bold political ideas and vital stories to all walks of life and arm the dreamers to demand the impossible. Founded in 2007 by a small group of people with decades of publishing, media, and organizing experience, we have sold millions of copies of our books, most often one at a time, face to face. We're old enough to know what we're doing and young enough to know what's at stake. Join us to create a better world.

PM Press
PO Box 23912
Oakland CA 94623
510-703-0327
www.pmpress.org

PM Press in Europe
europe@pmpress.org
www.pmpress.org.uk

FRIENDS OF PM

These are indisputably momentous times—the financial system is melting down globally and the Empire is stumbling. Now more than ever there is a vital need for radical ideas.

In the many years since its founding—and on a mere shoestring—PM Press has risen to the formidable challenge of publishing and distributing knowledge and entertainment for the struggles ahead. With hundreds of releases to date, we have published an impressive and stimulating array of literature, art, music, politics, and culture. Using every available medium, we've succeeded in connecting those hungry for ideas and information to those putting them into practice.

Friends of PM allows you to directly help impact, amplify, and revitalize the discourse and actions of radical writers, filmmakers, and artists. It provides us with a stable foundation from which we can build upon our early successes and provides a much-needed subsidy for the materials that can't necessarily pay their own way. You can help make that happen—and receive every new title automatically delivered to your door once a month—by joining as a Friend of PM Press. And, we'll throw in a free T-shirt when you sign up.

Here are your options (all receive a 50% discount on all webstore purchases):
- **$30 a month** Get all books and pamphlets
- **$40 a month** Get all PM Press releases (including CDs and DVDs)
- **$100 a month** Superstar—Everything plus PM merchandise and free downloads

For those who can't afford $30 or more a month, we have **Sustainer Rates** at $15, $10, and $5. Sustainers get a free PM Press T-shirt and a 50% discount on all purchases from our website.

Your Visa or Mastercard will be billed once a month, until you tell us to stop. Or until our efforts succeed in bringing the revolution around. Or the financial meltdown of Capital makes plastic redundant. Whichever comes first.

The Story of Crass

George Berger

ISBN: 978-1-60486-037-5
$20.00   304 pages

Crass was the anarcho-punk face of a revolutionary movement founded by radical thinkers and artists Penny Rimbaud, Gee Vaucher and Steve Ignorant. When punk ruled the waves, Crass waived the rules and took it further, putting out their own records, films and magazines and setting up a series of situationist pranks that were dutifully covered by the world's press. Not just another iconoclastic band, Crass was a musical, social and political phenomenon.

Commune dwellers who were rarely photographed and remained contemptuous of conventional pop stardom, their members explored and finally exhausted the possibilities of punk-led anarchy. They have at last collaborated on telling the whole Crass story, giving access to many never-before-seen photos and interviews.

"Lucid in recounting their dealings with freaks, coppers, and punks, the band's voices predominate, and that's for the best."
— *The Guardian*

"Thoroughly researched… chockful of fascinating revelations… It is, surprisingly, the first real history of the pioneers of anarcho-punk."
— *Classic Rock*

"They (Crass) sowed the ground for the return of serious anarchism in the early eighties."
— Jon Savage, *England's Dreaming*

Burning Britain: The History of UK Punk 1980–1984

Ian Glasper

ISBN: 978-1-60486-748-0
$24.95   416 pages

As the Seventies drew to a close and the media declared punk dead and buried, a whole new breed of band was emerging from the gutter. Harder and faster than their '76–'77 predecessors, not to mention more aggressive and political, the likes of Discharge, the Exploited, and G.B.H. were to prove not only more relevant but arguably just as influential.

Several years in the making and featuring hundreds of new interviews and photographs, *Burning Britain* is the true story of the UK punk scene from 1980 to 1984 told for the first time by the bands and record labels that created it. Covering the country region by region, author Ian Glasper profiles legendary bands like Vice Squad, Angelic Upstarts, Blitz, Anti-Nowhere League, Cockney Rejects, and the UK Subs as well as the more obscure groups like Xtract, The Skroteez, and Soldier Dolls.

The grim reality of being a teenage punk rocker in Thatcher's Britain resulted in some of the most primal and potent music ever committed to plastic. *Burning Britain* is the definitive overview of that previously overlooked era.

"Ian Glasper's chatty, engaging history follows the regional lines along which UK punk's 'second wave' scene divided, as well as talking about the record labels involved and what the main protagonists, from the Anti-Nowhere League to Vice Squad, are up to now."
—Iain Aitch, *Guardian*

"Glasper is thorough and democratic. He lets everyone speak, tell their own story, edits out the rambling and bullshit, and presents a fair picture of all the main bands from all over the UK and Ireland. Geographically divided up. It's an encyclopaedic but down-to-earth reference book, full of detail and anecdotes."
—Ged Babey, LouderThanWar.com

Spray Paint the Walls:
The Story of Black Flag

Stevie Chick

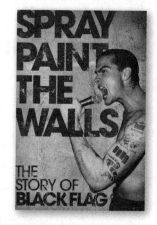

ISBN: 978-1-60486-418-2
$19.95   432 pages

Black Flag were the pioneers of American Hardcore, and this is their blood-spattered story. Formed in Hermosa Beach, California in 1978, for eight brutal years they made and played brilliant, ugly, no-holds-barred music on a self-appointed touring circuit of America's clubs, squats and community halls. They fought with everybody: the police, the record industry and even their own fans. They toured overseas on pennies a day and did it in beat-up trucks and vans.

Spray Paint the Walls tells Black Flag's story from the inside, drawing on exclusive interviews with the group's members, their contemporaries, and the bands they inspired. It's the story of Henry Rollins, and his journey from fan to iconic frontman. And it's the story of Greg Ginn, who turned his electronics company into one of the world's most influential independent record labels while leading Black Flag from punk's three-chord frenzy into heavy metal and free-jazz. Featuring over 30 photos of the band from Glen E. Friedman, Edward Colver, and others.

"Neither Greg Ginn nor Henry Rollins sat for interviews but their voices are included from earlier interviews, and more importantly Chuck Dukowski spoke to Chick—a first I believe. The story, laid out from the band's earliest practices in 1976 to its end ten years later, makes a far more dramatic book than the usual shelf-fillers with their stretch to make the empty stories of various chart-toppers sound exciting and crucial and against the odds."
—Joe Carducci, formerly of SST Records

"Here is an exhaustive prequel to, followed by a more balanced re-telling of, Rollins' Get in the Van journal, chronicling Flag's emergence in suburban Hermosa Beach, far from the trendy Hollywood scene (Germs, X, etc.) and how their ultra-harsh, hi-speed riffage sparked moshpit violence—initially fun, but soon aggravated by jocks and riot police. Greg Ginn, their aloof guitarist/slave-driver/ideologue dominates in absentia. Gradually, he fires everyone but Rollins, yet, his pan-American shoestring SST empire is relentlessly inspirational. A gory, gobsmacking read."
—Andrew Perry, MOJO

"Chick's analytical and in-depth biography of the progenitors of SoCal Hardcore builds up to a page-turning, scene-setting climax… Chick does a fine job of detailing the importance, influence and dedicated touring ethic of the band. Not to mention finally laying to rest the ludicrous but long-running Stalinesque punk rock opinion that of all Flag's diverse career output, only the material before Rollins joined was of any value."
—Alex Burrows, Classic Rock

Left of the Dial: Conversations with Punk Icons

David Ensminger

ISBN: 978-1-60486-641-4
$20.00   296 pages

Left of the Dial features interviews by musical journalist, folklorist, educator, and musician David Ensminger with leading figures of the punk underground: Ian MacKaye (Minor Threat/Fugazi), Jello Biafra (Dead Kennedys), Dave Dictor (MDC), and many more. Ensminger probes the legacy of punk's sometimes fuzzy political ideology, its ongoing DIY traditions, its rupture of cultural and social norms, its progressive media ecology, its transgenerational and transnational appeal, its pursuit of social justice, its hybrid musical nuances, and its sometimes ambivalent responses to queer identities, race relations, and its own history. Passionate, far-reaching, and fresh, these conversations illuminate punk's oral history with candor and humor.

Rather than focus on discographies and rehashed gig memories, the interviews aim to unveil the secret history of punk and hardcore ideologies and values, as understood by the performers. In addition, Ensminger has culled key graphics from his massive punk flyer collection to celebrate the visual history of the bands represented. The book also features rare photographs shot by Houston-based photographer Ben DeSoto during the heyday of punk and hardcore, which capture the movement's raw gusto, gritty physicality, and resilient determination.

Interviews include Peter Case (Nerves, Plimsouls), Captain Sensible (The Damned), Tony Kinman (The Dils), El Vez, Charlie Harper (UK Subs), The Deaf Club (an oral history of the landmark San Francisco club), Mike Palm (Agent Orange), Gregg Turner (Angry Samoans), Ian MacKaye (Minor Threat, Fugazi), Jello Biafra (Dead Kennedys), Gary Floyd (Dicks, Sister Double Happiness), Mike Watt (Minutemen, fIREHOSE), Shawn Stern (Youth Brigade), Kira Roessler (Black Flag, Dos), Jack Grisham (TSOL), Keith Morris (Circle Jerks, Off!) Fred "Freak" Smith (Beefeater), U-Ron Bondage (Really Red), Vic Bondi (Articles of Faith), Lisa Fancher (Frontier Records), Dave Dictor (MDC), and Thomas Barnett (Strike Anywhere).

"David Ensminger is the right mix of intellectual and real-ass emotional punk. He is a historian and has walked the life... I recommend everything this man is up to!"
—Dave Dictor, MDC

"David is one of the rare scene insiders who also has a depth of knowledge of the social and political context for the punk and hardcore moment. His love for the scene and understanding of its importance is unique, well-researched, and valuable."
—Vic Bondi, Articles of Faith

Punk Rock: An Oral History

John Robb
with a foreword by Henry Rollins

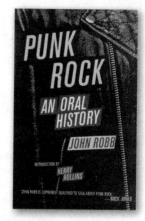

ISBN: 978-1-60486-005-4
$19.95   584 pages

With its own fashion, culture, and chaotic energy, punk rock boasted a do-it-yourself ethos that allowed anyone to take part. Vibrant and volatile, the punk scene left an extraordinary legacy of music and cultural change. John Robb talks to many of those who cultivated the movement, such as John Lydon, Lemmy, Siouxsie Sioux, Mick Jones, Chrissie Hynde, Malcolm McLaren, Henry Rollins, and Glen Matlock, weaving together their accounts to create a raw and unprecedented oral history of UK punk. All the main players are here: from The Clash to Crass, from The Sex Pistols to the Stranglers, from the UK Subs to Buzzcocks—over 150 interviews capture the excitement of the most thrilling wave of rock 'n' roll pop culture ever. Ranging from its widely debated roots in the late 1960s to its enduring influence on the bands, fashion, and culture of today, this history brings to life the energy and the anarchy as no other book has done.

"Its unique brand of energy helps make it a riot all its own."
—Harp Magazine

"John Robb is a great writer… and he is supremely qualified in my opinion to talk about punk rock."
—Mick Jones, The Clash

"John Robb is as punk rock as The Clash."
—Alan McGee

Barred for Life: How Black Flag's Iconic Logo Became Punk Rock's Secret Handshake

Stewart Dean Ebersole
with additional photographs by Jared Castaldi

ISBN: 978-1-60486-394-9
$24.95   328 pages

"The Bars represent me finding my people. We were like a tribe. Together we are strong whereas before we felt weak and ostracized."

Barred for Life is a photo documentary cataloging the legacy of Punk Rock pioneers Black Flag, through stories, interviews, and photographs of diehard fans who wear their iconic logo, The Bars, conspicuously tattooed upon their skin. Author Stewart Ebersole provides a personal narrative describing what made the existence of Punk Rock such an important facet of his and many other people's lives, and the role that Black Flag's actions and music played in soundtracking the ups and downs of living as cultural outsiders.

Stark black-and-white portraits provide visual testimony to the thesis that Black Flag's factual Punk-pioneering role and their hyper-distilled mythology are now more prevalent worldwide then when the band was in service. An extensive tour of North America and Western Europe documents dedicated fans bearing Bars-on-skin and other Black Flag iconography. Nearly four hundred "Barred" fans lined up, smiled/frowned for the camera, and issued their stories for the permanent record.

Barred for Life expands its own scope by presenting interviews with former Black Flag members and those close to the band. Interviews with alumni Dez Cadena, Ron Reyes, Kira Roessler, Keith Morris, and Chuck Dukowski, as well as photographers Glen E. Friedman and Ed Colver, and the man responsible for tattooing The Bars on more than a few Black Flag players, Rick Spellman, round out and spotlight aspects of Black Flag's vicious live performances, forward-thinking work ethic, and indisputable reputation for acting as both champions and iconoclastic destroyers of the Punk Rock culture they helped to create.

"Barred for Life is a book with heart. It also avoids the trap that similar single-subject photo books fall into. There's actually a narrative arc, thanks to a series of interviews with former band members interspersed throughout, telling the story of the band and its fans."
—BlackBook

Positive Force: More Than a Witness: 30 Years of Punk Politics In Action

ISBN: 978-1-60486-242-3
$19.95   180 minutes
DVD format: NTSC

Punk activist collective Positive Force DC emerged in 1985, rising from the creative, politically-charged ferment of DC punk's Revolution Summer. Born in a dynamic local scene sparked by Bad Brains, Minor Threat, and Rites of Spring, a handful of young activists also drew inspiration from UK anarcho-punks Crass and the original "Positive Force" band Seven Seconds to become one of the most long-lasting and influential exponents of punk politics. This feature-length film by Robin Bell skillfully mixes rare archival footage (including electrifying live performances from Fugazi, Bikini Kill, One Last Wish, Nation of Ulysses, Crispus Attucks, Anti-Flag, and more) with new interviews with key PF activists like co-founder Mark Andersen (co-author of *Dance of Days*) and supporters such as Ian MacKaye, Ted Leo, and Riot Grrrl co-founder Allison Wolfe. Covering a span of 30 years, *More Than a Witness* documents PF's Reagan-era origins, the creation of its communal house, FBI harassment, and the rise of a vibrant underground that burst into the mainstream amidst controversy over both the means and the ends of the movement.

The filmmakers' portion of the proceeds from the sale of the DVD will benefit the We Are Family senior outreach network.

Extras:

Wake Up! A Profile of Positive Force DC (28 minutes, 1991, a film by David Weinstein) A powerful snapshot of Positive Force at its early '90s peak, just before the eruption of Riot Grrrl and "Smells Like Teen Spirit," with a special focus on the role of the PF communal house.

Green Hair, Grey Hair (28 minutes, 2008, a film by Katrina Taylor & Rachell Williams) Award-winning short documentary that spotlights the unlikely—but transformative—alliance between inner-city seniors and young punk rockers fostered by PF's work with the "We Are Family" senior outreach network.

"Positive Force is the activist group that has helped define Washington, DC's legendary punk rock scene."
—Eric Brace, *Washington Post Weekend*

"Positive Force is an effort to recover the sense of community, ideals and purpose that had made the punk movement so inspiring."
—*SPIN*